Secrets of the VIKING NAVIGATORS

*How the Vikings used their amazing sunstones
and other techniques to cross the open ocean*

Leif K. Karlsen

*A sunstone
crystal*

★ ★ ★ ★
★   ★
STARPATH
www.starpathpublications.com

Digital composition and design by Marlin Greene, 3 Hats Design, Seattle
Cover painting by Leif K. Karlsen

ISBN 978-0-914025-61-0

Published by

Starpath Publications

3050 NW 63rd Street, Seattle, WA 98107

Manufactured in the United States of America

starpathpublications.com

10 9   8   7   6   5   4   3   2

CONTENTS

Part 3—Voyages of the Vikings Across the North Atlantic as Described in the Sagas... From the Navigator's Point of View.

Part 4—1000 Years Later

ACKNOWLEDGMENTS

Special thanks to:

June Garrett-Groshong, my wife. I acknowledge with sincere gratitude the assistance, support and encouragement throughout this project.

Gísli Arason and Ólafur Vilhjámsson, Höfn, Iceland

David Burch, PhD, Director of Starpath School of Navigation, Seattle, Washington, USA

Dr. Arne Emil Christensen, PhD, Director, Vikingships Museum, Bygdøy, Norway

Sea Captain Laurence Gellerman, Northwest Seaport, Seattle, Washington, USA

Drs. Sveinn Jakobsson and Aevar Petersen, Icelandic Institute of Natural History, Reykjavik, Iceland

Colin McDaniels, Seattle, Washington, USA

Commander Ólafur V. Sigurdsson, Icelandic Coast Guard, Iceland

Sea Captain Søren Thirslund, Maritime Museum, Kronberg, Denmark

іптродистіоп

Over one thousand years ago, in open, hand-built wooden ships powered by massive, hand-loomed sails, the Vikings navigated the challenging waters of the North Atlantic. This was during the "Viking Age," approximately from the year 800 to the year 1050, when the Vikings of Norway were Europe's most renowned sailors. Their explorations first reached the Shetland Islands and the Faeroe Islands, then Iceland, then Greenland, and, finally, the shores of the North American continent. How the Vikings managed to navigate these vast distances, time and time again, without sextant, magnetic compass, charts, or even an accurate timepiece, is the subject of this book.

I have used the original Viking sagas as a beginning reference guide. These sagas were ancient stories, first handed down orally from generation to generation, and not written down by scholars until the thirteenth and early fourteenth centuries. According to these sagas, the Vikings used whales, swells, birds, the stars and the wind as clues to aid in navigation. Keep in mind that the scholars writing these descriptions were not navigators. I am convinced that the Vikings also employed techniques and devices, born of necessity and their ingenuity, that did not get described in the sagas.

I believe one of the unknown navigational aids used by the Viking navigators was the Solarsteinn or "sunstone." Sunstones, clear crystals found predominantly in Iceland, are often mentioned in the sagas as prized possessions, ranked on a par with a fine stud horse as an indicator of wealth. My research has convinced me that the Vikings used these naturally-occurring crystals to locate the position of the sun when the sun was completely obscured by the frequent fog and low clouds typical in the North Atlantic.

In a natural world that is filled with rare and exquisite examples of incredible uniqueness, sunstones defy the rational mind.

1

Sunstones are roughly the shape of a three-dimensional parallelogram. All sunstones, without exception, have the same geometric shape and same angularity. Take a large sunstone and break it into smaller pieces and you will have pieces with the exact same angles and geometry as the original. Additionally, every face of the stone has a tilt of 11.5 degrees. The geometry of this unique crystal and how it is used as a navigational aid will be examined in detail later on in this book.

Without knowing the precise time of day, it is impossible to determine longitudinal position. Longitudes are the earth's north-south axes. So the Vikings navigated only by latitudes (the east-west axes) and, in doing so, reached their chosen destinations with surprising accuracy. Following a more or less straight line east or west is called "latitude sailing" and this was the technique employed by the Vikings.

The latitudes at which the Vikings sailed and many of the places the Vikings settled correspond with the latitudes (declinations) of four "zenith stars" in the Big Dipper as they appeared in the year 1000. Included in the book are charts of the principal navigational stars as they appeared a millennium ago. Steering by the stars was also an important navigation method, as was the "shadow pin" technique of finding true north when the sun was available. These are also discussed.

The book begins with a narrative that will give the reader the opportunity to share an open ocean passage with a Viking merchant seaman and his crew. Their conversations and observations serve to introduce the secrets of Viking navigation.

Leif K. Karlsen, Port Orchard, WA, USA

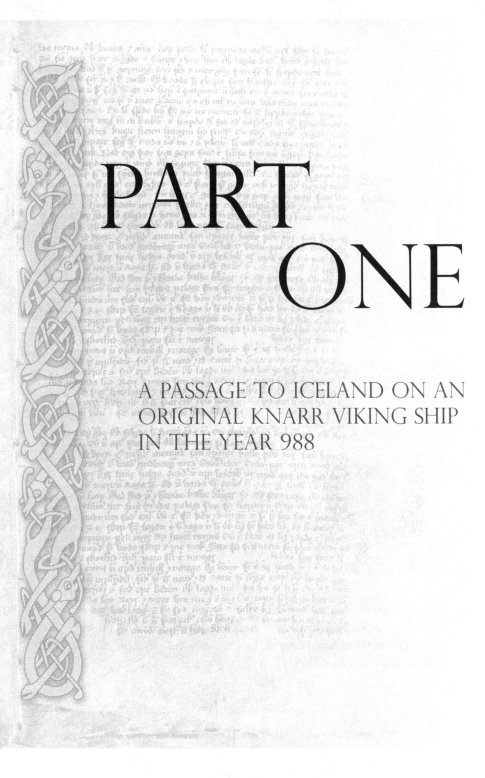

PART ONE

A PASSAGE TO ICELAND ON AN
ORIGINAL KNARR VIKING SHIP
IN THE YEAR 988

The history of the Vikings is linked to their mastery of the sea. Ships were the basis of all Viking activity: war, trade, or exploration. This is the story of a voyage as might have been, told by a young Viking merchant seaman, on his first passage from his home in Norway to Iceland.

# CHAPTER ONE

I Become the Owner of My Own Ship

My name is Hákon Leifursson. I have just completed the first passage from my homeland to Iceland on my own ship. I've made the passage ten times on my father's ship since I was fifteen, but this time on my own ship I made the passage. But let me start at the beginning and tell you the story.

My father is a merchant and trader who still sails his own ship from our home port of Trondheim, Norway. He is well respected and knows the sea better than anyone else I know. He taught me so much for the past ten years that my head is full of his voice saying, "Do this if this happens—do that if the wind changes." We came back to our home port of Trondheim from a very successful voyage to Iceland in the late summer of last year, number 987. He told me then he had decided this was a good time for me to have my own ship because I had learned all he could teach me, and he could tell that I was ready to be independent. I was happy to have his blessing to be the captain of my own ship.

I went to the boatbuilders in Sunndalen who had been building ships for generations and had a reputation for building strong ships of the best quality. Both my father and some of our best friends had their ships built there. I talked things over with the boatbuilder Sverre Sunndalen. We decided that they should build for me a *hafship*, a seagoing vessel called a *knarr*.

The ship was to be built for cargo and seaworthiness, and to be a good heavy-weather sailer. It would have an open cargo hold amidships with decking at both ends, but with little protection for the people onboard. The *knarr*

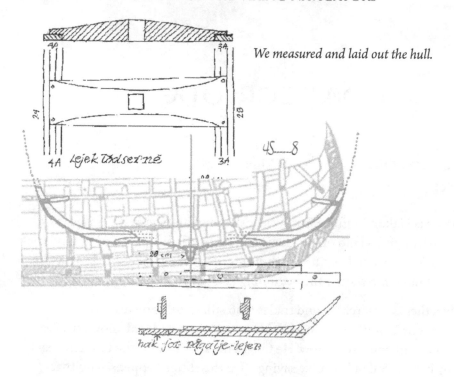

We measured and laid out the hull.

would also be fitted with two sets of oars fore and aft, mainly to be used for rowing in and out of the harbors. Since I wanted to expand on the size of my father's ship, I asked them if they could make my ship even larger. They said they could; it would be the largest ship they had built in Sunndalen.

And so my ship was started in Sunndalen. This is where the finest trees for boatbuilding are to be found. The timber was selected by Sverre Sunndalen using trees from his own farm. I talked with the boatbuilders and discussed whether to use oak or pine for the planking. They decided to use pine, both for lightness and for flexibility on a ship of this large size. Tall pine trees with straight grain and without low branches were used for the planking. The trees were split for the planking using wedges, and then carefully shaped with axes and scraping tools. As they were finished, the planks were stored under water to keep them green and workable until they were needed.

The frames and curved pieces of the ship were formed by following the grain of specially selected trunks and crooked limbs of oak trees. These were trees where the burden of winter snow and ice had bent the trunks and limbs into natural curves. Pieces with the right curves were carefully selected. This made for pieces of greater strength, which were easier to finish to curved shapes than if they were bent from straight-grained wood. The curved fore-and-aft stems were carved from a single piece of oak from an old bent trunk. The keelson, keel, and frames were also made out of oak. All of these pieces were carefully shaped by hand.

Old, bent branches were used for curved parts.

We chose pine planking for lightness and flexibility for the hull.

7

We measured and laid out the lengths for the hull. The *knarr* would be *beamy*, a very strong ship, 54 feet long, with a 15 foot beam, and an extra high freeboard. Height amidships was to be 6 feet. There were 12 planks on each side, with the widest being about 20 inches.

The keel was laid last autumn. After a busy winter the boatbuilder and his two sons had the *knarr* hull built and ready for launching in the early spring. I watched and eagerly helped as it was taking shape, and I learned many things about my ship by watching as it was being constructed. I learned how before the overlapping planks were riveted together, a string of wool is soaked in pine tar and placed between the planks to keep the hull watertight. I often picked up the tools to get the feel of how to shape the wood. Sunndalen's son showed me how to use the adz and broadax, so that now I can replace a section of wood if it gets damaged.

Boatbuilding yard at Sunndalen.

The side rudder used for steering was mounted on the starboard quarter aft by a rope through the upper planking and pivoted on a boss lower down, about halfway down between the upper planking and the keel. The steering oar is controlled by an *athwartship* tiller.

The *knarr's* hull was a masterpiece, sitting there with several fresh thin coats of pine-tar on the outside. All in all, I could see it was going to be a beautiful ship.

Since Sverre Sunndalen's farm is located inland several miles from the fjord, we had to transport the vessel on a special wagon pulled by horses down to the fjord where it was launched. People from near and far came to see the launching of the biggest vessel ever built in Sunndalen.

After the launching, the ship was named after the national bird of Iceland: the Geirfálki (Gyrfalcon). She was now ready to be rigged and outfitted for her first voyage to Iceland.

The *siglutre* (mast) was made of pine, 42 feet high. All the lines were attached to the mast before it was raised. The mast was *stepped* (raised) and the yardarm fitted, held to the mast by a *rakki*, a piece of wood shaped like a horseshoe used to keep the yardarm close to the mast. The standing rigging was kept simple, with a forestay to the bow, the backstay to double as a halyard to hoist and lower sail. The *shrouds*—four on each side of the mast— were fastened to the frames.

I purchased the finest *siglu* (square sail) to be had from a sailmaker in Trondheim who imports *wadmal*, the best sail making material available, from Iceland. *Wadmal* is made from specially selected sheep's wool, using the long outer hairs of the fleece for strength and durability. The lanolin is left in the fleece. The wool is spun and tightly woven into long strips, which are then sewn together and oiled to make the sail windtight and water resistant. The total area for my sail was about 120 square yards.

The lines for the rigging are all made of tarred hemp. The smaller lines are made from horsehair. After several hours of rigging and pulling lines, the sail was securely attached to the yardarm, and finally the ship was ready to sail.

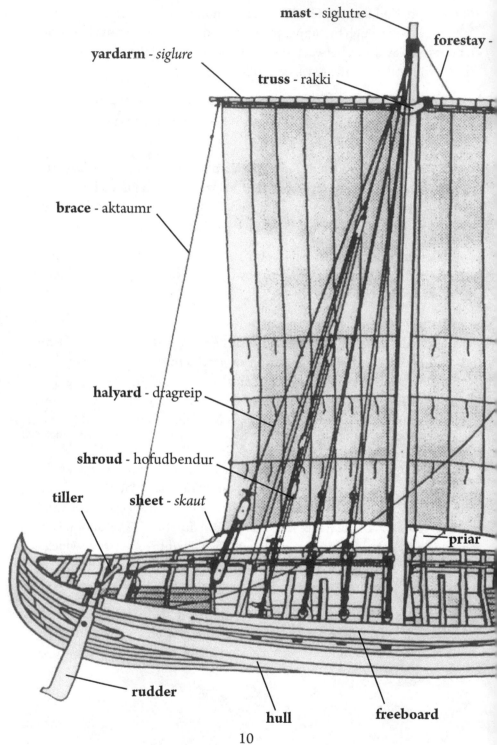

mast - siglutre

forestay -

yardarm - *siglure*

truss - rakki

brace - aktaumr

halyard - dragreip

shroud - hofudbendur

tiller

sheet - *skaut*

priar

rudder

hull

freeboard

Materials and Dimensions of "Geirfalki"

Length:	54 feet
Beam:	15 feet
Freeboard amidship:	6 feet
Mast height:	42 feet
Hull material:	Pine planking
Deck material:	Pine boards
Sail area:	120 sq. yards
Sail material:	Wadmal
Lines rigging	Tarred hemp
Small lines	Horsehair

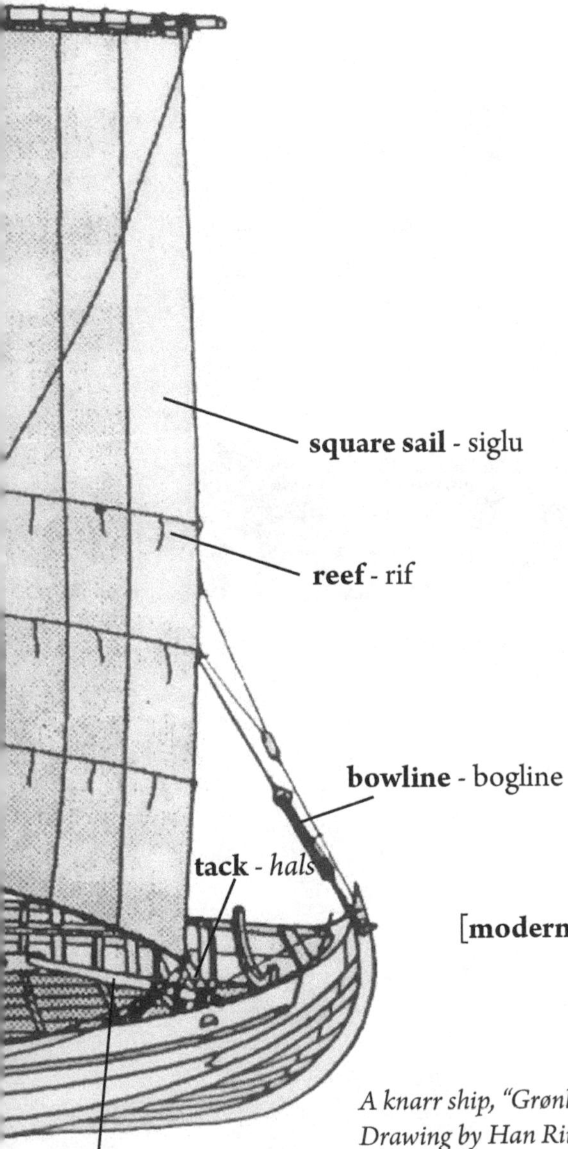

square sail - siglu

reef - rif

bowline - bogline

tack - *hals*

[**modern english** - old Norse]

tackpole - *beitiás*

*A knarr ship, "Grønlandsknarren" (The Greenlandsknarr).
Drawing by Han Riishede with kind permission from
the Vikingship Museum in Roskilde, Denmark. The vessel
and rigging are discussed in Chapter 10.*

11

"I name you 'Geirfálki'—may you be as fast as the bird you are named for."

# CHAPTER TWO

Seeking a Crew and Cargo for the Trip

First I sailed my new ship home to Trondheim, Norway, to look for crew and cargo for the passage to Iceland. My friends and family were the temporary crew. They all left the ship in Trondheim, except my younger brother Kaare, who wanted to make his first passage to Iceland with me.

Everyone brought goods with them for trade in the city, since Trondheim is a major marketplace. Merchants gathered from distant lands to set up their booths to sell their wares. We all had a great time seeing the array of merchandise on hand and gathering news from other lands.

Trondheim is a good place to find a crew for the voyage to Iceland. It is customary for many Icelandic merchants and seamen to spend the winters here, since ships do not make the voyage to Iceland in the late fall or winter due to the severe weather. The crewmen would be looking for passage back to Iceland in the spring when I planned to sail.

I could hear my father's advice in my head, "The main thing is to be a good captain, keep your ship in good shape, for then a capable crew will join you." I knew I had a good ship and that I was known as a good captain and extraordinary seaman. So off I boldly went, the proud new ship owner and captain, to the market place in Trondheim to announce my planned voyage to a few merchants. All I said was, "I have a new ship and I am looking for cargo and a good crew to sail to Iceland." It was but a short wait before capable men started showing up to volunteer, and before long I had my first crew.

Sigurbjörn, an Icelander, was the first to join. Sigurbjörn had been a friend for a long time. We first met on my father's ship when I first went to sea years ago. Sigurbjörn said he was now ready to teach me many of the business strategies that had made him such a successful merchant. Sigurbjörn would bring to Trondheim dried and smoked fish from Iceland. With the profit from the sale in the market place in Trondheim he would purchase kegs of mead and barrels of wine to take back to Iceland. He had established a profitable market for wine and mead in Reykjavik.

Sigurbjörn knew of three cousins, Thorvik, Baird, and Thord who were looking for passage back to their home in Iceland. Sigurbjörn said he would find them and let them know there was a good ship leaving for Iceland soon. The three cousins had spent the winter in Norway with the Norwegian part of their family. Their Norwegian relatives were blacksmiths, so the cousins had traded *wadmal* cloth they brought over from Iceland for the excellent tools made by their family. They were going back home with the iron tools for the market in Reykjavik.

Next I found Arn and Oláfur in the market place. They were both Norwegian merchants who had vast holdings of forested land. I told them that timber was always in great demand in Iceland, and would fetch a good

The route of the "Geirfálki"
Sunndalen—place of construction to Trondheim—one day.
Trondheim, Norway to Horn, Iceland—eight days and 725 nautical miles.
Then on to Reykjavik on the western side—just under four days.

14

price. There were no trees growing in Iceland that could make good boats or houses. All of the lumber had to be imported. Arn and Oláfur thought this was a good idea for establishing a business, and agreed to go on this voyage to Iceland. They said they felt very lucky to have met with me, such a well-known seaman, and to have this opportunity to join my ship. This would be their first trip to Iceland, and they were looking forward to a good summer there. They had many friends in Iceland who had moved from Trondheim, and they wanted to visit them all.

Last to join the crew were Gudmund and Egil, and Egil's friend Geir. Gudmund and Egil were father and son. They had heard the gossip in the market that there was a good ship looking for crew. They came to the harbor, found my ship, and offered their services. They had brought falcons to Norway from Iceland, and now needed to return home. They had traded the falcons for flour. They knew that flour was always needed in Iceland, and they anticipated making a good profit. I could tell from their appearance that they were strong and capable men and I welcomed them aboard.

Geir was a handsome young trader from Iceland. This had been his first trip to Norway. He brought fine walrus ivory that he had obtained in a trade with a Greenland merchant he had met in Reykjavik. He had traded the ivory in the Trondheim market for fine and delicate purple cloth from a travelling merchant who had gotten it from a far away land he wouldn't name. The merchant would only say that the cloth came from a land by the sea where purple dye is made from seashells. Geir thought that cloth of this rare quality would fetch a good profit in Iceland. These merchants not only served as the crew, they were also responsible for their own cargo. Under the captain's guidance, a merchant brings his cargo aboard, secures it, watches over it at sea to prevent any damage to the merchandise, and unloads it at the destination.

The youngest crew member was my brother Kaare Leifursson who was coming along to learn the merchant trade. I had also promised to teach him the secrets of navigation which I had learned from our father.

Everyone paid for their passage and cargo space in *wadmal*, silver, or both. I was, like most merchants and captains, equipped with a small pair of scales for weighing the silver when the deal was made. I told Kaare that I preferred *wadmal* for payment, because Norwegian merchants considered coins of value only as a source of metal. In most cases, they melted down the silver coins for metal to make jewelry.

In addition to the working crew, I also had a newlywed couple, Trygve from Iceland, and Ögn from Norway, joining as passengers to Iceland, along with their five sheep which they had received as a wedding gift. Many captains refuse to allow livestock onboard their ship. They think it attracts bad luck. This is part of the Old Ways. I don't believe livestock attracts anything but strong odors, so I let them come along.

A newlywed couple joined as passengers to Iceland, along with their five sheep which, they received as a wedding gift.

# chapter three

"Geirfálki" Departs on Her First Voyage

Several days before departure, all the navigational gear was tested and the references were verified for latitude 64° North. The height of Polaris, the "North Star," was noted, and the height of the low twilight stars was measured and marked on a reference board held at arm's length. A bearing of the sun at sunrise and sunset was also taken with the horizon board. All the lines and ropes were checked and tested for strength. The anchor and anchor line were tested. The entire rigging was given a good going over, including the rigging blocks. At last the sail was secured to the *siglure* (yardarm), and finally the sail was hoisted. For two days the ship went through trial runs without any major trouble. Only a few small adjustments to the length of the shrouds were needed. The ship, the crew, and the captain were now ready for the first voyage of the "Geirfálki."

I called everyone together and announced, "When the weather is favorable, I would like to leave as soon as possible. Make all preparations for the voyage."

One part of the Old Ways that I halfway believe in is the casting of the Runes. The ones called "Christians" discouraged any part of the Old Ways. Many people who prefer the Old Ways are moving to Iceland, or on to Greenland, so they can continue their preferred way of life without scorn.

My mother always insisted on casting the Runes before allowing my father to pick the day he would leave. She intended to offer me the same protection. The Runes are a collection of twenty-four symbols engraved in small pieces of stone or wood. The pieces are randomly drawn from inside a pouch where the collection is kept. For my passage my mother drew:

> "*raiðo*"—which means journey, pilgrimage, change, destiny, quest, progress, life lessons.
> "*wunjo*"—for success in any endeavor, to motivate, to complete the task at hand.
> "*jera*"—change, cycle turning, reward, motion, productivity, inevitable development.

She was very excited about the results of the Runes and said that she was now sure the Gods were smiling on us; I now had her blessing to leave.

After saying goodbye to my family I had to turn to final preparation for the voyage. First, I made sure the sunstone was onboard and well protected, due to its fragile nature. Food, water, and the necessary supplies were taken onboard. Extra lines were stored. Oiled wool, cloth suitable for mending sails, was also taken onboard, along with a large number of needles, plenty of thread and cord, and a supply of nails, both spikes and rivets. We needed supplies and shipwright tools in case we had to make emergency repairs to the ship, at sea or in port. We took carpenter tools such as broadax, adz, wooden breast auger with metal bits for boring holes in timber, extra axes, knives, chisels for log splitting, wedges, hammers and tongs used in forging iron nails, and not to forget the bailing buckets. The tools were oiled well and wrapped in hide to keep the iron from rusting.

Casting the Runes.

Maritime law requires the captain to make the ship ready so thoroughly that it is fully fit for sea, with all its gear and enough fresh water for the passage. We had five casks of water onboard. One cask held about enough water for six men for the expected duration of this voyage, so I had more than enough water for the minimum requirement. I also brought food aboard which was mostly dried or smoked fish, and smoked meat, as well as some vegetables and fruit which was dried, salted or pickled. The crewmembers brought additional preserved food onboard.

A ship laden in accordance with maritime law, when it is divided into fifths, will have three parts submerged and two above the water line, measured amidships. This is a measurement of the maximum amount of cargo that was safe for a ship to carry. I knew the common cause for ships going down in rough weather was from overloading. I have seen other crews loading deck cargo until their ship could hardly float. I was very careful not to overload the ship, and I explained this reasoning to the merchant crew.

We spent a full day carefully loading and securing our cargo. First we loaded the timber to be used for houses and boat building. Then came the barrels of flour, the kegs of mead and wine and the iron hand tools. Geir's fine cloth could be damaged by water, so it was wrapped in layers of *wadmal* and then covered with hides. These tight packages were then stowed in watertight trunks. When all the cargo was onboard and secured, personal belongings were brought on board. The ship's *færing*, a four-oared rowboat was stored upside down on top of the cargo and secured. Late in the day, Trygve and Ögn brought their sheep onboard with some hay for bedding and fodder. At last all the cargo was loaded and we were ready to sail.

By now it was early April. I had been waiting for a day with favorable weather and wind conditions. I couldn't take an untried ship out any earlier than April because the frequency of storms is greater in the early spring, and I was not certain how well the ship would handle in a storm.

The next morning brought the bright, early April day I had been waiting for; I decided it was the right time to leave Trondheim and head for Horn, located on the southeast coast of Iceland.

Everything loose was stored away and lashed securely to prevent it from shifting. The crew was present, the passengers were all excited, anticipating getting underway. Thankfully the sheep were calm. The gangplank was taken in and stowed away. The lines were let go and the ship began to float free at last.

As the ship slowly pulled away from the dock in a gentle breeze, the crew discovered that Geir was missing. He was still on the dock saying goodbye to his girlfriend. Everybody yelled, "Come on Geir, run, you can make it." Geir came running as the ship moved slowly away from the dock. With great effort Geir jumped from the dock to the ship. He was able to grab hold of the sternpost and hang on. Thorvik and Thord grabbed him by the coat and the seat of his pants and pulled him onboard. He landed on deck headfirst but unharmed. Egil remarked that Geir couldn't be hurt because he had landed on his hard head. Geir felt very foolish in front of the whole crew. I told him that he was neither the first nor the last seaman to almost miss the ship, and he shouldn't be embarrassed.

The ship began to float away from the dock—free at last.

After leaving the dock in Trondheim, we sailed out the Trondheimsfjord using known landmarks as guide. With a variable wind we headed out, passing the island of Hitra on the port side, then into the Frohavet and out into the North Sea. Using the Halten area as a departure point, I set the course due west to cross the ocean, following roughly the 64th parallel, heading for Horn, Iceland, which is also at latitude 64° North. Total distance to sail was about 725 nautical miles. After the first hour, the weather was still nice, but the wind had picked up and shifted to northeast at about 20 knots. The ship was making good speed.

That evening I showed my brother Kaare how to get a bearing of the sun while we still could see the landmarks on shore. On the horizon board for latitude 64° North, I had all the bearings carved for the summer months from March to September, on the 21st of each month, and another set of bearings for each seventh day. All these bearings were prepared before the voyage using the information from voyages made in previous years.

I reminded my brother, "You have to remember Kaare, there are three times a day that you can get a reference bearing of the sun: at sunrise, noon, and again at sunset. With these reference bearings you check the wind and swell directions to steer by. The more often you get a bearing the more accurate the course becomes. Always stay on top of things. You never know when the weather will change. With a good reference bearing you will at least have the wind and the swell to steer by."

During the first night, around midnight, the wind decreased and shifted and became northerly; the sea was moderate, and the ship moved along on a starboard tack making good speed.

Of the thirteen people onboard, the nine merchants were standing watches, three men on each watch. As the captain, I was always available and expected to take charge when needed. As well as learning the secrets of navigation, my brother Kaare was learning seamanship by taking turns at the tiller and doing other chores. The two passengers, Trygve and Ögn, helped out when needed. Trygve was an experienced seaman and carpenter, and Ögn was well acquainted with the sea from her experience helping her father on his fishing boat. Standing orders were that in rough weather all hands would be turned to, each man would take a turn at the tiller, handle the lines, man the sail, bail, and perform any other functions necessary for the safety of the ship.

21

At sunset, the ship was still on a good heading west. After dark I was able to get a bearing of Polaris, the "North Star." I told the man at the tiller to hold the bow towards a low star on the western sky, and to keep Polaris on the starboard beam. Since the stars changed direction as they moved across the sky, it was later necessary to shift to another star to steer by, again using Polaris for orientation. It was common knowledge that higher northern stars rise north of due east and set north of due west.

I knew the height of a certain star in the Big Dipper which just skimmed the horizon at twilight. I had marked this distance on a reference board before leaving home. If the distance increased it meant we were set farther north, a decrease meant we were farther south than our desired course. From the observation of Polaris and the measurement of the distance above the horizon of the skimming star, I could tell that we were still holding a good course west. Later, I would explain these secrets to my brother.

Fog drifted in during the night. The next morning the horizon was obscured by a fog bank, but there was a clear blue spot of sky overhead. The rising sun could not be seen, so we could not take a direct bearing of the sun. Now I was happy that I had the sunstone with me. The sunstone would point to the rising sun through the fog. I went up to the bow with my brother and took out the sunstone, and with it I found the exact bearing of the sun. Then we used the horizon board and aligned it with the sunstone's bearing. The horizon board showed the sun's true bearing and the desired course was read from it. Kaare was impressed. He had heard rumors of this stone, but didn't know that they really worked. I just held the stone up toward the heavens, looked through it, rotated it a little, and had the bearing. It seemed magical. I promised Kaare that I would soon teach him how to use this remarkable stone.

With the wind on the starboard side all night, I discovered that we had been set to port. I decided to compensate by steering up to starboard before we got too far off course. The weather was still nice, the sea was moderate, and the wind was still from the north at about 15 knots. The "Geirfálki" was flying like a falcon; we were making good headway.

At noon on the second day, an update of the heading was made by using the shadow pin. I told Kaare how to find true north each day at noon by using the shadow pin. "The basis for this is simple, just compare the length of an afternoon shadow with that of the morning shadow. You have to be extra careful when you are taking bearings of the sun. Avoid looking up at the sun directly, but instead keep track of the shadow. This way you avoid going blind! Some time before noon you set up a steady course. A cloud on the horizon, wind, or swell direction from a previous sun bearing, or a landmark will work for the duration of the observation. Also remember that the heading must be the same for the two readings: the one before noon and the one after noon. Place the shadow pin with the sharp point up, perpendicular to the horizon in the center of a flat board that must be kept level with the horizon. Mark the first point where the tip of the pin's shadow falls and draw a circle through this point with the base of the pin at its center. A string from the base of the shadow pin to the first mark will be used for this. In the afternoon when the shadow again touches the circle, you mark the second point.

Midway between the two marked points lies the meridian of the observer. This will be the north-south line. Now you connect the first and the second mark and this will give you a west-east line, and that's all there is to it."

Setting up the shadow pin on the horizon board.

Kaare replied, "Thanks for teaching me all this. I know, Hákon, that navigation is a secret known only to the navigator." I quietly answered, "Without the secret of how to navigate, the captain, or the navigator, is powerless, and there could easily be mutiny onboard, so what I am teaching you now is strictly between us. These secrets hold the safety of the ship and crew, and assure the authority of the captain and the navigator."

Kaare then asked me how we would know our direction in bad weather. I told him to be patient as he was sure to find out before too many days passed.

Looking for the direction of swell to steer by.

# CHAPTER FOUR

Secrets of Using the Sunstone

By now, everything onboard had settled down to a routine. If a crewmember was not on watch, steering, splicing lines, or doing other chores, he was free to rest or play games—some were learning business tricks from each other. Sigurbjörn had already made fourteen voyages between Norway and Iceland. With his experience and knowledge, he was often asked for advice about trading. Trygve and Ögn were usually tending to the sheep, trying to keep them calm. So far they were pretty relaxed and didn't even smell bad.

There were no provisions made on the vessel for sleeping quarters. People onboard slept on the foredeck, afterdeck, and sometimes in the cargo hold, or any space that was available and somewhat dry. They slept wrapped in wool blankets, covered with hide for warmth and, hopefully, to keep the water out. Nor is there modesty aboard a Viking ship, but because of the woman Ögn being aboard, I had ordered everyone to answer Nature's call back at the stern behind a small screen we had rigged from spare planking.

It was easy to see that it was spring. The nights were quickly getting shorter and shorter with only a few hours of darkness, and I knew that soon the stars would disappear completely until next fall. I reminded Kaare, "Whenever you see Polaris, be sure you get a bearing. At twilight, check out the distance above the horizon of the skimmimg star against the height we recorded at home. You can also verify our heading by keeping Polaris off the starboard beam."

Just before sunrise I told Kaare, "We have to get a good bearing of the sun this morning because there is a large fog bank coming in on the horizon. It looks like the fog will be with us for a while, so be sure you check the wind and swell direction at the same time. At least we will have something to steer by when we are in the fog."

In early morning the fog began to encircle the ship. There was still blue sky overhead, but nothing could be seen for any distance in any direction from the ship. I spoke privately to Kaare, saying, "Let's go up on the bow away from everybody, and I will show you more secrets of the sunstone." When we were alone, I began the lesson. I said, "First of all, in order to use the sunstone you must place a small spot of pine tar on top of the stone, on the side which faces towards the sky. When you are using the crystal for the first time, place a small wooden pointer along either one of the longest sides. This will be a guide for which side to point toward the brightest part of the sky. Then you must hold the stone overhead and view the stone from underneath. Notice the double image of the black dot? Now, line up the pointer towards the brightest part of the sky. When you rotate the stone slightly back and forth, holding it flat, you will see that one spot fades and the other becomes darker. When the two images appear to be equal in value, note the position of the stone and the direction of the pointer. This is the true bearing to the sun.

The stone is very accurate. A good place to practice taking bearings with the stone is when you are ashore and you can compare the bearing with the known direction to the sun. The thickness of the crystal is very important. The thicker the crystal the better the separation of the black mark. One more thing, the bearings are best at sunrise and sunset, when the sun is slightly below the horizon."

Kaare was amazed that we could find the hidden sun. He asked, "When we get to Iceland, do you know anybody who will sell or trade a stone to me?" I answered, "Yes, I have a very good friend, Gisli, in the Horn area. He is the same man I got my sunstone from. We will try to get a stone like mine, as thick and as clear as possible. As I said before, the information I have given you here is strictly between us." Kaare replied, "I remember, and thank you for showing me how the sunstone works." I took another long look at the white mist and thought to myself, "Now we are ready for fog—with a true bearing of the sun and the wind and swell direction, we will be all set for a while, but I would rather do without the fog."

By midmorning the fog was so dense we could not see the horizon. I called the crew together and told them, "We must use the swell direction to steer by." The wind was from the north at about two knots. A lookout was placed on the bow and Egil took the first turn on the tiller.

By the next day there was still no improvement in the weather. We were still using the southwest swell to steer by; we could not get an update on our course at noon due to the sun still being hidden.

The sunstone needs a dot of black pine tar on top.

It is said that the first chip that the boat builder cuts from the stem tells the fate of the boat. But many boat builders do not want to learn the fate of the boat and turn their heads away when they strike the first blow.

# CHAPTER FIVE

Changeable Weather is Something You Can Depend On

By the middle of the day the visibility was getting worse. We were using the swell from the southwest to steer by. My father had told me, "When thinking about weather, change is something you can depend on." On days four and five nothing changed; it was still foggy and overcast with little wind. We could not get a bearing to update our course. Shortly the wind picked up to five knots from the north. With the East Iceland current on the starboard bow, and the wind on the starboard beam, I reckoned that the ship was set to port. I gave orders to Thorvik, "Change course a bit to starboard and we will keep it there for a while, and be sure you watch the swell carefully after the course change."

In the evening of the fifth day it became dead calm. I said to the crew, "Drop the sail, we are not going anywhere right now except drifting, and we are being set south by the East Iceland current. Everybody can turn in and try to get some sleep except Thorvik, Baird, and Arn. They will be on watch."

During the night the wind increased and the fog cleared. Early morning on the sixth day before daylight, everybody was awakened and turned to for duty. The sail was hoisted again. It was still dark enough to see the Big Dipper. With the Big Dipper in sight it was easy to locate Polaris. I called Kaare, saying to him, "I want to again show you how to locate Polaris, since this is always the pointer to the north, it is the best guide in the sky. Remember, you will have no trouble finding Polaris if you use Dubhe and Merak, the two stars on the cup end of the Big Dipper. They point to Polaris; that's why these two stars are called 'the pointers.' You draw an imaginary line between them and extend the line straight up. The distance to Polaris is five times the distance between the pointing stars. This is how you locate Polaris, which is the last star on the handle of the Little Dipper. By looking at the postion of Polaris off the beam of the ship, we can tell that our heading has gradually shifted—we are off course. Later I will show you how to get more accurate direction from Polaris using the Little Dipper stars as guides."

I then assigned Kaare to the tiller with these orders, "Head up to starboard and watch the position of Polaris so we can get back on our westerly course again. Remember what I told you last time about keeping Polaris on the starboard beam and holding the bow towards a low star in the western sky." The wind was about 20 knots from the northeast and the ship was flying along. The sail was set on a broad reach. I shouted aloud, "Now we are sailing, this is more like it."

Before noon on the sixth day the sun was visible again and Kaare set up the shadow pin for the noon observation. I guided him through the procedure as before. The sea had started to build, so we rigged a gimble for the shadow pin board by fastening it to the top of a wooden stick which had a lead weight at the bottom. We hung the stick with lines so it could swing free above the deck. In this way, the board remained level as the ship moved under it. The sky was clear and it looked good for the duration of the noon bearing.

Baird was at the tiller. He had long experience at sea. He knew how to keep a good steady course using a low stationary cloud close to the horizon to steer by. From the noon bearing, we could see that we again were off course a bit. We compensated by heading up to starboard.

Shortly after the noon observation the clouds began to move in fast. The wind shifted to the north and increased to near gale force in the stronger gusts. The waves began to build. They were getting higher and longer. Soon the ship began taking water over the side. From time to time the sea was snapping at the railing and occasionally green sea came onboard. As captain, I ordered everyone to "turn to," some to handle the sail and the rest to bail. I changed the course to southwest to keep the ship from rolling too much against the swells. The ship's speed increased in the strong wind. I knew it was not safe to sail at exactly the same speed as the waves traveled. If we did so the ship would ride on top of a wave and lose steerage because the steering oar would come out of the water. At the same time the ship would also lose some of it's normal stability. I decided we had to reduce the speed of the ship by taking one reef in the sail.

Thord relieved Baird at the tiller. Thord was another great seaman with long experience in the Norway-Iceland trade. Arn, Oláfur, Thorvik, Baird, and Kaare took places to handle the sail. Gudmund, Egil, Geir, and Sigurbjörn bailed the ship. Suddenly a huge wave hit the ship, came in over the rail and smashed two of the water kegs together, breaking the side of one and spilling the fresh water into the cargo area. Nothing else seemed to be damaged.

It was hard to keep the torches lit. We had to carry one torch under a hide shelter when we move around the ship.

Trygve and Ögn were with the sheep. They tried to keep them calm. They had to rope them together and then hold the rope tightly to keep the sheep from being injured by the wild motion of the ship. With all the water sloshing about it was difficult for everybody to work and move around. Gudmund, Egil, Geir, and Sigurbjörn bailed frantically to keep the water from rising any more.

I decided to take one more reef in the sail. It was now around midnight, and the weather was overcast with rain. I shouted out, "Everybody must stay awake tonight in case the bad weather worsens." Lucky for us it did not.

By daylight, the wind had abated, the skies were clearing, but the seas were confused. When the wind is steady, waves have a regular pattern, but the changing wind creates confusion until a new pattern develops on the sea's surface. In the meantime the ship's motion will be rough. The crew did their best to hold the ship to a steady course.

By late morning, the weather was much calmer and so was the sea. I gave orders to take out the two reefs in the sail, and told the men to resume their normal watches at sea. I directed all those not on duty should try to get some well-deserved sleep.

31

I called my brother and we made a full inspection to see whether there was any other damage from the large waves that had smashed into the ship. Luckily, the only damage was the broken water keg. I was pleased with my ship. It had handled very well in rough weather, the true test of a seaworthy vessel.

Kaare said he would like to change into dry clothes. He was soaked to the skin with the cold North Atlantic waters. I nodded in agreement, saying, "It is impossible to stay dry on an open ship like this. Also, you should turn in and get some sleep. When you are at sea, you should rest and sleep at every opportunity, because you never know when the weather will change. You might be up for days without sleep due to storms and rough weather."

I went to Geir, who was at the tiller, and said, "I will turn in and try to get some sleep. If there is any change in the weather, or if you should see the sun, give me a call."

Just before noon, the sky cleared and the sun came out. Geir woke me to say the weather had changed. He told me the weather was much better, and best of all, the sea was getting calmer.

At noon on the seventh day we got an update on our heading by using the shadow pin. From the updated heading we determined the direction of the swell and wind. I decided to use the swell direction as a reference to steer by for the rest of the day until sunset.

During the afternoon the wind shifted to southwest at about 17 knots. The ship was now on a port tack, moving along at a fairly good speed in moderate seas. Activity onboard was now settling down to routine again. It was Arn's turn at the tiller, with Egil on the bow as lookout, and Geir splicing lines for the sail. Thorvik was busy carving and making handles for his knives that he would sell as soon as he got to Iceland. Oláfur, Gudmund, and Baird were adjusting the sail, Trygve and Kaare adjusting the *beitiás*, *belly priars*, and the bowline. Sigurbjörn and Thord were mending an extra sail in case we needed it. At sea another task that must be done seems to wash aboard the ship with every wave.

# CHAPTER SIX

We Complete Our First Open Ocean Crossing

Everybody could feel that we were getting closer to land. The crew had already seen birds flying back and forth to their colony all day long. They were fulmars, roaming the open seas hundreds of miles away from their colony. I told the crew, "Soon you will be able to spot the puffins, murres, and other kinds of birds making several trips to and from the colony every day. Most activity takes place in the early morning hours. The puffins, murres, kittiwakes, and the gannets are especially noted for travelling in small flocks back and forth from the feeding grounds. This is the first sign that land is up ahead. The next sign will be the landmark we all are looking for, namely the Vatnajökull glacier."

Trygve was the lookout and Ögn went up to the bow to be with him. This was her first trip to the new home she and Trygve were going to build together. She could hardly wait to see the big glacier and the new land she had heard so much about. After a few days with rough weather, everybody was looking forward to seeing land, and according to my estimation land should show up soon. Then all of a sudden, there was a cry from Trygve and Ögn. They had spotted the snow cap of Iceland's highest point, the Hvannadalshnúkur at 6,950 feet. It is located on the south side of the Vatnajökull glacier and projects 900 feet above the Oraefajökull, a glacial tongue that projects into the sea. In clear weather, the Hvannadalshnúkur can be seen from the deck of a *knarr*, just on the horizon, about 86 nautical miles away.

The sun would still be up for a few hours more, and the snow cap was a beautiful sight to see. Everybody was crowding the bow of the ship to watch this beautiful mountain, majestically floating on the horizon as the ship moved toward our destination.

I had seen it many times onboard my father's ship, but there was a special feeling inside when I saw it from the deck of my own ship. Seeing the mountain rise out of the water always made me wonder. I knew it didn't really rise out of the water like it appeared to. The only other possibility that I could think of was that the ocean was curved, like a big ball, and that made the mountain appear to rise as we sailed closer. My father and most of the other captains agreed with this notion.

After a bit of daydreaming, looking at the snow-capped Vatnajökull glacier, I set the course west, heading for the Örafajökull glacier and Horn. The weather was perfect, nice and clear with the wind still from the southwest at just about 14 knots. The *knarr* was on a port tack. I had the crew constantly adjusting and trimming the sail to find the best angle and fullness for perfor-

After days at sea we at last saw the peak of Hvannadalshnúkur, slowly rising higher and higher out of the water, as we made for land.

mance. This allowed me to also teach my brother Kaare how to set and adjust the sail. Baird was at the tiller; Arn was on lookout. Geir was on standby to relieve Baird at the tiller when it was his turn. The rest of the crew was resting.

I reminded Arn, "Keep a sharp lookout for the Vesturhorn Mountain. It will be our guide to the harbor. It should show up on the starboard bow." After a while Arn saw the Vesturhorn Mountain and he told me immediately. I said to Baird, "Change course to starboard and steer straight for the Vesturhorn."

Shortly after sunset it was time for Geir to take the tiller. Arn went on standby and Baird on lookout. I knew from experience that the coastal and tidal currents move in a clockwise direction around the coast of Iceland, and I told Geir to head for the east side of the Vesturhorn because the current would set us in a southwesterly direction during the night to come.

The wind decreased to about ten knots and the sail was adjusted accordingly. The sea condition was about two feet. I said to Kaare, "It looks like we will make it into the harbor at about daybreak." It was time for watch change again, Sigurbjörn at the tiller, Thord to bow as lookout, and Thorvik on standby. Everybody else was either sleeping or resting. It was a welcomed, peaceful night.

I did not want to take any chances when it came to departure or arrival. As the sun came up over the horizon, the *knarr* was slowly sailing towards the entrance to Horn with just enough wind for steerage. A low fog bank was seen dead ahead at the entrance. I sent Gudmund and Kaare to the bow as lookouts. Egil and Ólafur were also sent to the bow with the hand lead to measure the depth in shallow waters. The lead consists of a line with a weight at one end that is dropped in the water. The line is marked with strips of leather—two fathoms from the lead with two strips of leather, three fathoms from the lead with three strips of leather, and so forth. We also have another lead for deep-sea measure—the deep-sea lead—which the sailors call "dipsey." It has much heavier weights and is a longer and stronger line. Different markings are used on the dipsey, such as different colored strips of cloth. The fogbank did not last very long and the leads were not required so they were stowed away.

On the morning of the eighth day of the voyage, just after sunrise, we arrived at Horn harbor. Shortly after arrival, Trygve and Ögn got off the ship with their sheep. Everybody said goodbye to Trygve and Ögn, and wished them good luck in building their new home. Trygve´s father Agnar was on the dock to meet them, and to take delivery of the sheep. Agnar said, "I have been watching you for a long time coming in to the harbor." Trygve and Ögn would move in with Agnar while they built their own place. Agnar had told Trygve he could use the material of a shipwreck that he had stored at his farm to start their new home. Timber was hard to come by in Iceland and people salvaged any and all wood, including shipwrecks and driftwood. Imported timber from Norway was very expensive.

Until we arrived in Reykjavik, the rest of the crew and the cargo were to stay onboard "Geirfálki." We were all happy to be safely tied to the dock for a short rest before the next passage began.

A short time later Gisli came racing down to the ship on horseback. I was happy to again see my old friend. It was almost a year since I had last met Gisli in Iceland. I introduced my younger brother Kaare and the rest of the crew to Gisli. Everyone was full of questions about the latest gossip in Horn, and happy to have a day to relax and enjoy some lively conversation.

As soon as we were alone, I said to Gisli, "Kaare is interested in obtaining a good sunstone, like the one I bought from you last year. Can we get one?" Gisli answered, "Sure, we can take a ride up into the mountain tomorrow morning. I will meet you here and bring the horses. Then we can ride up into the Hoffell area and look for a good stone for Kaare."

"Geirfálki" was finally quiet. I was sitting on the gangplank when the harbor chief came up to me and said, "You are following in your father's wake, Hákon Leifursson. Come to my house for the evening. There is a story you must hear." And so I spent the evening hearing the telling of the story, and will relate the story he told to me. It is about the voyage of Bjarni Herjulfsson, a merchant seaman who is a friend of my father.

Bjarni Herjulfsson would spend his summers in travel between Norway and Iceland, carrying cargo on the large *knarr* ship he owned. His custom is to return to Iceland each fall to spend the winter with his father, Herjulf. In the fall just passed, he had come to Eyrarbakki, his father's port in southwest Iceland, from Norway. When he arrived he was told that his father had left Iceland with a large party of settlers bound for the new land discovered by Eirik the Red, which Eirik had named Greenland.

Now Bjarni was greatly surprised and distressed, and instead of unloading his ship and dismissing the crew, he announced that his intention was to spend the winter with his father. He told his crew that he was prepared to leave at once and find Greenland if they would go with him. They all replied that they would go with him, and so they departed.

They intended to sail into the Greenland sea to the west, following the way Eirik had gone, but the fair winds failed. Fog and north winds prevailed for many days and they had no idea which way they were carried. When the sun finally came out again, and they could get a bearing, they hoisted sail and headed west. After a day they sighted land, but Bjarni didn't think it fit the description of Greenland that he had heard, so they only sailed close and didn't go ashore. They could see the land was vast and wooded, with low hillocks. They then sailed away to the northeast and after two days they sighted another land. Bjarni said, "Like the first, neither is this land Greenland." There were no glaciers, and the land was wooded. They again turned from the land without going ashore and sailed out to the open sea. A strong southwesterly wind carried them for three days to a third land. When the crew again asked Bjarni if they should not go ashore he replied, "No, this land looks unprofitable." He was anxious to find his father as the sailing season was by now almost over. Now they once again hoisted sail without going ashore and headed northeast. On the fourth day of sailing they sighted land again. This time Bjarni said, "This looks like Greenland according to what I have been told. We will steer to that land." They headed straight to the headland and soon saw a ship on the shore. With the good help of Njörd, who rules the wind and sea, Bjarni had landed at the very place in Greenland where his father had settled, and he spent that evening in his father's house. Now many captains are talking saying, "Bjarni has discovered a wonderful land with forest and plenty far beyond what we have in Greenland, and he did not even look around." There is much talk among the other captains about completing the exploration of this land.

I listened to the story with amazement. Could there be land to the west beyond Greenland? I, myself, had never meet Bjarni Herjulfsson, but I knew him from my father's knowing. He was a good captain and an honest man.

I thanked my host for the telling of such a wonderful story and excused myself to sleep. It was a long time before I could get the words of the voyage of Bjarni out of my head and visions of vast wooded shorelines kept me awake.

CHAPTER SEVEN

To the Source of the Sunstones

The following day Gisli showed up on horseback with two extra horses, one for Kaare and one for me. Gisli was proud of his horses. He told everybody about the Icelandic horses. The first settlers brought the Icelandic horses over in open boats from Norway. The Icelandic horse is small and very sturdy. The horses were used as a sign of power, and often offered as a special gift. When the owner of a horse died, his horse was put down and buried with him. This was another part of the Old Ways. The Icelandic horse is best known for its five gaits. These are the walk, trot, gallop, and the two distinctive gaits: pace and toelt. Toelt is a running walk. It is a gait of four equal beats, with only one foot touching the ground at any one time, which can escalate swiftly from slight motion to great speed.

Gisli told everyone the story of Odin's horse. Odin's horse, Sleipner, had eight legs. Gisli said if you watch an Icelandic horse from a distance running quickly, it looks like the horse has eight legs instead of four, just like Odin's horse. After telling the stories, Gisli called out to us, "Let's get going for the sunstone."

We rode off into the Hoffell Mountain where Gisli had found a vein of Iceland spar on his farm. Gisli was sure that they could find a perfect sunstone. We had plenty of food and water with us, so we spent a long, relaxing day on the mountain. The long days brought plenty of daylight so we did not have to hurry back to the ship. After looking around for a while, we found the perfect stone for Kaare, an absolutely crystal-clear stone. Gisli said "This is a gift from my land for Kaare," In the late evening we returned to the ship. Gisli promised, "I will stop by the ship tomorrow before you sail for Reykjavik to wish you luck."

It was now the tenth day since we had left Norway. Fresh water, stores, and additional cargo was taken onboard in the morning. The cargo was *wadmal* and hides bound for Norway. I was also expecting two passengers to join us before noon.

As we were making ready to leave Horn for Reykjavik, Egil asked me if we could follow the coast closely to Reykjavik because he was in a hurry to get there to sell his goods. I snapped, "No, because the weather is unsettled this time of the year and we have to watch it very carefully." Egil had some angry words for me as he was almost desperate to reach Reykjavik ahead of another merchant who was bringing over similar goods on another ship. I told him forcefully, "I am in charge of the ship, cargo, and the safety of all the people onboard. This time of the year we will give the coast between Horn and Vest-

The Icelandic horse is highly valued.

mannaeyjar a wide berth, just close enough to use the mountains between Horn and Reykjavik for landmarks. There can be no discussion about this." This was Egil's first voyage away from home and he had little experience with the ways of the sea. He walked away very unhappy after this confrontation.

Soon after this confrontation two passengers arrived, two brothers, both farmers from the Reykjavik area. The older brother's name was Eirik and the younger was named Asbjörn. They had been looking for good farmland to settle around the Hornafjördur area and were now going back to Reykjavik to get their families.

The crew was just about ready to take in the gangway and let go the mooring lines when Gisli came riding up. He had been delayed while trying to cross a river with extra high floodwater. He had had trouble finding a place to get across. Gisli came onboard and said goodbye and wished everybody a safe voyage to Reykjavik. It was a sign of the bond between us that he had gone to great effort to come and say goodbye as he had promised.

With a storm brewing, we had to steer clear of the coast.

# chapter eight

On to Reykjavik

We left Horn on the 11th day from the beginning of our voyage. The sky was overcast, but visibility was good with the wind from the north at 3 to 5 knots. The first watch was set with Sigurbjörn at the tiller, Thorvik on lookout, and Thord on standby. As soon as we were outside the harbor the wind started to pick up, and so did the sea. I wondered if this was a sign of things to come. In the afternoon the wind and the sea kept increasing, and my feeling about bad weather between Horn and the Vestmannaeyjar was right. Instead of sailing close to the coast, I set the course south and headed out into the open waters in order to minimize the risk of being blown back on shore.

I called everybody to the afterdeck area and explained the situation. I told everyone, "A storm is brewing. It is too dangerous to go back to Horn. We might run out of maneuvering area. It looks like we are in for a rough ride. We will ride out the storm by running before it, that is by having the wind coming from the stern." I next assigned duties. "I need the best men on the tiller. Baird will take the first turn, then Thorvik, Sigurbjörn, and Arn, in that order. With the sea at the stern, the ship will have the tendency to be forced broadside to the waves, which could break over the side and fill the ship. That is why I need a good man at the tiller at all times, to hold steady and not allow the ship to turn broadside. I will also take a turn if and when needed. The main thing to worry about is to keep the ship from broaching."

Everybody was turned to on deck. The *priars* were tightened to flatten the sail and get the belly out. The *siglure* was lowered and three reefs were taken in the sail. Wind was still increasing and the sea was building. The speed of the ship was also increasing to the point of danger. It was close to being out of control. I yelled over the wind, "Drop the sail all the way and secure it." There was little change in speed. Then I shouted, "Take the spare sail we have onboard and use it as a droug." The lines in the sail were then secured to a heavy mooring line and in turn secured to the stern of the ship. The entire sail was dropped over the stern. The speed of the ship was slowed down considerably. In the meantime, the ship had taken several waves of green water over the stern, and everybody was bailing for their life.

The ship itself was taking the gale quite well, but everybody's life was in the hands of the man at the tiller. Just a slight mistake and the ship would turn broadside and it all would be over.

At times there were monstrous waves rolling in from the stern area. Several times when it seemed one was going to break in over the stern of the ship, it would go down right behind the stern, just a few feet away. In rough seas the speed should be reduced and the sea be allowed to come to the stern; that is the only chance to make it through.

A ship and crew are always tested in foul weather.

After a while the waves dropped a little and the ship was riding much better. Less and less green sea came up to the stern. By early afternoon both the wind and the sea were subsiding. I told the crew, "Hoist the sail and use three reefs in the sail, and keep the sail as flat as possible. We will try this for awhile, but be ready to drop the sail if the speed picks up too much."

By late afternoon the sky cleared up and the sun had come out. I then thanked everyone for the hard work during the gale. "I am glad we made it, thanks to the good seamen we have onboard who all know how to steer in wild weather." I remembered a short saying that old-time sailors made up to encourage them through squalls and storms:

"The sharper the blast, the sooner it's past."

And of course everybody and everything was soaking wet from the gale. Some of the men were still bailing in the cargo hold. I commented, "I am glad the sheep are not onboard on this passage. It's difficult to keep animals calm in such a gale."

Now that he had experienced the storm, Egil understood what I had meant and the reason why I did not choose to follow close to the coast all the way to Reykjavik. He apologized for his temper and said he was grateful that I was the captain.

Mostly everybody had a dry change of clothes in their sleeping bags, which were made of hide, or at least they had a dry bed to sleep in. There was still a lot of bailing and cleaning up to do, and everybody was working hard to get it over with so they all could get some well deserved rest and sleep.

Shortly after midnight, early morning of the 13th day, the wind shifted to the east at about 20 knots, and the combined sea and swell was about 12 feet. I called the crew together and announced, "Time for a course change to southwest." The ship was moving along, still with three reefs in the sail on a broad reach.

I explained to the crew, "If the weather stays like this we will change course shortly to due west and take advantage of the coastal current, which is flowing in a clockwise direction around Iceland." The watches were set again. The first watch was Thord at the tiller, Ólafur on lookout, and Egil on standby. The others took a long deserved rest.

Just before sunrise the course was changed to west. The wind was still from the east at 20 knots. The reefs were taken out and the sail was hoisted all the way up. At once you could feel the ship picking up speed. The sail was adjusted to running before the wind. This is the condition when the shape of the *knarr* hull brings the ship up out of the water due to the air that is forced under the hull. Behind the ship at the stern I could see a trail of air bubbles on the surface.

Before noon Sigurbjörn, Kaare, and Geir, who now were on watch, saw the ice of Mýrdalsjökull glistening off the starboard bow. The Mýrdalsjökull is a gigantic glacier lying on the volcano Katla. At 4,970 feet, it can be seen far out to sea off the coast of southwestern Iceland. By the late afternoon the Mýrdalsjökull was on the starboard beam, and the Eyafjalljökull, a second glacial peak, was also seen forward on the starboard bow.

Sometime after midnight, the Heimaey Island in the Vestmannaeyjar was abeam, just visible in the moonlight. Again we had a wind change, this time to the southwest at about 15 knots. The sea was moderate. The course was changed to northwest. The sail was adjusted and again we were running before the wind. I kept this course until we were abeam Reykjanes Point where I changed course to north. The sail was adjusted accordingly to a broad reach; the wind about 7 knots the sea about 2 feet. At this point the ship was sailing close to shore and Kaare was studying the landscape very carefully and discussing what he saw with Arn. Kaare turned to me and said, "It looks like they have had a tremendous fire in this area." Since this was Kaare's first trip to Iceland, everything was new to him, including the lava flows. I said, "It is not from fire, it is a lava flow from a volcano. You will see this in a lot of places in Iceland."

As the ship was approaching Reykjavik, I told everyone a little about its history. Reykjavik was the first place in Iceland to be settled. The first settler, a chieftain from western Norway named Ingólfur Arnarson, arrived in Iceland with his family and dependents around 874. He and his blood brother Hjörleifur had to escape from Norway because of some trouble they had encountered there. Hjörleifur settled near the present town of Vik but was murdered by his servants shortly after they arrived. Ingólfur let the Gods choose his homestead. He tossed his high-seat pillars overboard and built his farm at the place where the gods chose to bring the pillars ashore. He called the place Reykjavik, or "Smokey Bay" due to the steam rising from nearby thermal vents in the ground. He was lucky to find his pillars quickly. I have heard of some people searching for years to locate their pillars.

We arrived safely in Reykjavik harbor shortly after sunrise on the 15th day and dropped the anchor. Lots of people turned out for our arrival. They must have spotted the ship early and passed the word that a *knarr*-type ship was heading for the harbor. Merchants, cargo, and news from Norway were always a big event here. Many of the people have family and friends who still live in Norway.

The ship's *færing* (rowboat) was removed from the top of the cargo and lowered into the sea. I went ashore with Kaare and Thorvik to clear the ship with the town officials before the passengers and crew members could go ashore and before we started unloading the cargo. The harbor master told me there was no toll for men from Norway and the ship was cleared to start discharging cargo. We rowed back to the ship and prepared to unload the cargo. There was only one small dock in the harbor; the water near the dock at low tide was too shallow for my fully loaded *knarr*. I decided to stay at anchor and wait for the high tide before we approached the dock with the ship.

In the meantime we started unloading what cargo we could get ashore. The cargo that was acquired in Horn, but destined for Norway, was now removed from the cargo hold, stored on deck and covered with hides for the time being. Everybody took part in the unloading of the cargo. Geir's two watertight trunks were loaded in the *færing* together with a few of Sigurbjörn's kegs of mead and wine barrels. They had to make three trips in the rowboat to get all of the mead and wine barrels ashore. Arn and Ólafur did the

The 'high-seat pillars' of wood form the main support in the center of halls and sanctuaries. They were decorated with carving of significance to the owner.

shuttling between the "Geirfálki" and shore. Friends, relatives and towns-people handled it from there. And so it went until most of the cargo, except the timber, was sent ashore. Luckily for everybody there was no damage to anything; everything was in excellent condition, thanks to the extra effort we put into packing and securing the cargo.

Next came the time to get all of the timber ashore. I decided it would be easier to stay at anchor away from the dock and finish the discharging from there, rather than to tie up to the dock. The timber was thrown overboard log by log, then tied together into small rafts and towed ashore. It required making many trips with the *færing*. Men with horses were waiting to pull the timber high up onto the shore where it would stay until the buyers came to bid on the timber and haul it away.

The two passengers, Eirik and Asbjörn, were taken ashore by Geir. Before they left the ship they told me that next time they are in the Horn area and need to get back to Reykjavik, they will use horses because never were they so scared as they were in that gale. I reassured them by saying, "It is not like this most of the time, and you are welcome aboard my ship anytime. Remember, on horseback it makes for a long trip across Iceland." Everyone then paid for their passage and cargo space as we had agreed.

Gudmund and his son Egil were met by their family and had a happy reunion. They then went up to the market to see how much they could get in trade or sale for the flour they had brought back from Norway. Thorvik also went up to the market to sell his knives with the beautifully hand-carved handles.

Thord, Geir and Baird said goodbye and went home with no plans beyond taking it easy for a while. If they decided to go back to Norway this year, they said they would look for me when I came back to Reykjavik in the late summer. They said they would rather sail with me than with anyone else.

Arn and Ólafur planned to sail back to Norway with Kaare and me. They stayed in one of the little temporary dwellings by the harbor that are used by seafarers from abroad for short stays, and by men waiting for passage out of Iceland. If foreigners wintered over in Iceland, they usually took lodging in permanent households rather than staying in those little huts.

For the first time in several days I had time to look back at the days just completed. The "Geirfálki" had performed like the majestic sailing ship she was. I had managed to deliver the crew and cargo safely and had been paid well for the effort. I was already planning how I would start seeking cargo for the return trip to Norway. If I could leave by late in April, I would be able to make two more trips before the weather got too rough.

I then thought about the stories I had heard in the harbor at Horn about the land in the far west, the land Bjarni Herjolfsson discovered a few years ago, while looking for Greenland. If the land really was vast beyond belief, with forest that stretched forever, abundant with game and birds of every kind, then we must go there. Many captains from Iceland and Greenland are angry that Bjarni didn't learn something more about the place he discovered. I think that if I came upon such a land I would explore it for sure.

Viking coins were usually silver and mostly melted down to make jewelry.

The timbers extending above the hull at the bow and stern were used to align the ship with points on the horizon, with low stars, and with cloud formations for an aid in holding a heading.

CHAPTER NINE

Returning to Norway

Kaare and I were invited to stay with Sigurbjörn until it was time to sail in late April. After a few days rest we went to the market place to get the latest news. We also inquired about the possibility for getting full cargo for my return trip to Norway. It shouldn't be too difficult to get a full load and new crew, since I had found out that my ship was one of the first to arrive in Reykjavik so far this spring, and all of the merchants who had wintered over in Iceland were eager to travel and get their cargo to the markets in Norway. I wanted to make two more round trips before late autumn.

At the market place, I was approached by two merchants, Tryggve and Björn, both Norwegians, who came here last year and were now ready to go back to Trondheim with cargo. Björn had *wadmal*, wool, three falcons, and hides to be shipped from Reykjavik. Tryggve had smoked and dried fish stored at Eyrar and Vestmannaeyjar. The Vestmannaeyjar are a group of sixteen very small islands located off the mainland's south coast; Eyrar is a small port further up the coast. They both asked me if I had space aboard for their cargo. I said, "Yes, I can take care of it right away as soon as I get the rest of the crew for the voyage. One more thing, right now I'm at the anchorage, but I will shift to the dock tomorrow morning and we can start loading then. Right now the ship's cargo hold is empty, so there is no reason to wait for the high tide." Björn said, "I know of two very good seaman who are looking for passage home to Norway. I will contact them for you if you like, and we can meet here this afternoon."

Later in the afternoon I met with Björn and his friends, Eirik and Per and made a deal with them. They could work their way home and either pay for or bring their own food. They agreed to pay for the food.

After all this good news, I looked for my men, Kaare, Arn and Ólafur. Being Reykjavik is such a small place, I had no trouble locating them. I told them we have more cargo waiting for us; all we have to do is go and pick it up. First we would sail to the small port, Eyrar, located on the southwest coast not too far from here. Then we would go to Vestmannaeyjar Islands to pick up the rest of the cargo. Then we are ready to sail back to Trondheim in Norway. After I told them all this they were happy and eager to set sail for new places. This was all brand new for my brother Kaare, Arn and Ólafur and they could hardly wait to get going. I told everyone to meet on the ship tomorrow morning to get the ship moved to the dock so we could start loading Björn's cargo. At the same time we would get the ship ready for the return trip. We had to check the sail, lines, blocks anchor lines and bailers.

A couple of small cargo ships at the dock.

We needed to fill up the water casks and provide food enough to supplement the supplies that were brought on board by the crew for the voyage to the Vestmannaeyjar Islands. I told Sigurbjörn that we were leaving the day after tomorrow for Eyrar, then to Vestmannaeyjar to top off the cargo before heading to Norway. Sigurbjörn said, "I will stop by tomorrow afternoon to wish you a safe passage."

The following day the crew came on board with their personal belongings and were ready to work. First they hauled up the anchor. Then they rowed the ship to the dock, tied up the ship using our mooring lines, and started loading Björn's cargo of *wadmal*, wool, falcons, and hides. This cargo was stored so that it could easily be moved to accommodate additional cargo. The falcons' cages were secured and covered on the afterdeck close to the steering oar, so the man at the tiller could keep an eye on them. It turned out there was plenty of space left for Tryggve's cargo of dried and smoked fish, and space to re-stow the cargo which we had picked up in Horn on the way over.

In the afternoon Sigurbjörn came aboard and stayed for a while. He said, "It did not take you long to get a full cargo for your trip back to Norway. The merchants really liked you and your fast ship; it's the main topic of conversation in the town. Have a safe trip home and return quickly to Iceland."

Late that afternoon all of the cargo was on board. It was secured and covered in case of rain and to protect it from sea spray. The *færing* was once again stowed upside down on top of the cargo and secured with lines. Kaare and I made a full inspection of the cargo and ship before we turned in for the night.

In the early morning, when the sun was just beginning to rise, the ship was made ready to sail for Eyrar. I called out, "Wake up everybody! The weather is favorable and we will be underway as soon as possible. Kaare will take the first turn at the tiller. I will be available during the day to take a turn at the tiller as needed. Arn, Tryggve and Per will take the first watch when we get to Garðskagi, on the Reykjanes penninsula."

The gangplank was hauled aboard and stowed away. The lines were let go and the ship majestically began to move slowly away from the dock under sail. We kept the oars ready in case we needed them in a hurry. The course was set west, following the coastline.

The wind was from the north at about six knots and the sea was calm. The sail was set for *half-vind*, the condition when the wind is coming directly on the beam of the ship. I told Kaare to keep this course for a while. The watches will be set after the next course change at the headland off the point of Garðskagi. About halfway to the Garðskagi I said to Kaare, "I will take a turn at the tiller for a while and see how she handles in this kind of weather with this cargo. Since we will be using coastal navigation to get to our next two ports, this will be a good time for you to practice taking sun bearings and to practice coastal and celestial navigation. We will be using known landmarks such as headlands, glaciers, and mountains for our coastal navigational references. This will also be a good time for you to practice finding the directions from the sun. Start when we get to Garðskagi. The new course will be south. It will not be too late to take an observation. The sun still has a way to go before it is in the south, and the ship is steady as a rock and no gimbal is required. Let me know this afternoon about how it worked out."

Perfect weather for coastal sailing.

At the Garðskagi I changed the course to due south with the wind still from the north at about ten knots, and the sea was at about two feet. With the course change, the sail was adjusted to running before the wind. The speed picked up and the Geirfálki became alive. The ship was heading for Reykjanes, the westernmost point of southwest Iceland.

I told the first watch to turn to. Arn took the tiller, Tryggve went to the bow as lookout and Per was on standby to adjust the sail if needed. I said, "I will tell you a short story about Eyrar, the place we are headed for. This is the place Bjarni Herjolfsson sailed from when he was headed for Greenland and got far off course to the west, blown by a north wind and lost in fog. That is when he discovered the vast new western land that many people are talking about. Herjolf Bardarson, Bjarni's father, had already left Iceland with Eirik the Red and several hundred other settlers to colonize Greenland. Bjarni had just returned from a trip to Norway with cargo. The Horn harbormaster told me about how Bjarni found his way back to Greenland, when the sun came out again. He got his bearings and found his way to Herjolfsness, Greenland, where his father had settled, to the very harbor. I never met Bjarni, but my father knows him quite well from their meetings throughout the years at ports they both visited. My father says Bjarni is a good sailor—I think he is a bad explorer."

Arn remarked about the weather, "This weather is perfect for coastal sailing. The wind is with us, the sky is clear, the temperature is right. The sky is full of sea birds going back and forth between land and the sea, picking up food for their young ones. Even the whales are very active. Spring is definitely with us." Tryggve joined Arn in the conversation. "Just wait until we get abeam of Hafnaberg Cliff. You will see birds all over the sky." I said, "At Reykjanes point we will change our course to east, and head straight for Eyrar. If the weather stays like it is, we will have a very good passage." At Reykjanes the course was changed to due east to follow the coast all the way to Eyrar. The wind was still from the north and increased to about 20 knots. The sea was about 3 to 5 feet. When the course was changed the sail was also changed for *half-vind*, I said, "I need both watches to turn to and set the sail for the new course. Kaare will take the tiller. Tryggve, Per, and Eirik, move the *beitiás* to the port side and secure the tack to it. Also make fast the bowline. Arn, adjust the *priars*, Ólafur and Björn adjust the braces and the sheet." When making a major course change in strong wind I liked to be on the safe side and have all hands helping.

After the course change the men returned to normal duty. The second watch took over. I asked Kaare, "How did your bearing turn out? Were you able to find true north by the sun?" Kaare answered, "I almost forgot to keep watch on the shadow to make a mark when the shadow hit the circle the second time. Like you said, this was a good place to practice taking a bearing while the ship was steady and on a north-south course. The bearing came out just right. I verified it by comparing it to the north-south coastline. Thanks again for teaching me the secret of the sun shadow bearing."

It was soon time for the first watch to take over again. All of a sudden, Tryggve yelled out from the bow, "I can see the harbor of Eyrar off the port bow." I told Per to change course to port, a northeast heading, and steer straight for the entrance of the harbor. Once inside the harbor, we went straight to the dock and tied up. I said, "Even with the coastal current against us, we still made a fast passage. The distance from Reykjavik to Eyrar is about 92 nautical miles."

The sun had yet to set, so we had plenty of time to set up camp ashore for the night. I told the men, "When we go ashore for the night we need to bring food, and something to drink besides mead, and pots and pans to cook with for tonight and tomorrow morning. Hopefully we can catch some fresh fish or a couple of seabirds for breakfast."

We all went ashore and set up camp. We put up two big tents for the eight men, so there was plenty of room for everybody. After the meal it was time for stories to be told and poems to be composed. Viking seamen love poetry, and they compose beautiful stories in rhyme. The men enjoyed sitting around the fire in the evening and having a friendly competition for the best poem. Before they settled down for the night I said, "I would like to get an early start in the morning to load the cargo so we can reach Heimaey, Vestmannaeyjar sometime in the afternoon."

After a good night's sleep, and a good breakfast of fresh fish and seabirds that Arn and Eirik had luckily caught that morning, we all turned to. Half of the men started dismantling the camp and stored everything back on board. In most cases the men knew what they were supposed to do without me having to give them orders. The rest of the men started with Tryggve's cargo of smoked and dried fish and *wadmal*. The fish had to be stored as far away from the other cargo as possible due to the smell, even though the other cargo was well wrapped.

I used to think it was strange that with all of the fish available in Norway, that there would be a need to bring in more fish. Norway's markets are famous for the good quality of salt-dried and smoked fish, and people came from all over Europe to buy it, so there is never enough fish to supply the demand.

Loading and securing the cargo went fast. We were ready to sail long before the sun was in the south. The distance between Eyrar and Heimaey is about 37 nautical miles. I said, "Let's get underway. The weather looks

Seabirds are abundant along the coast.

favorable, except for the overcast sky. The wind was shifting about and gusting, not good for sailing out of the harbor. We will row out of this harbor and set the sail when we are well away from shore. The course will be southeast, the wind is from the northwest at about 15 knots. There will be no watches set on this short run. Everybody will take turns on the tiller and lookout. The rest will be on standby and turn to as needed. Haul in the gangplank and take in the lines. Per, take the tiller and Kaare go to the bow for lookout. Arn, go on standby to drop anchor if we get blown off course toward the shore. The rest of the crew take the oars."

Despite the size of a *knarr* ship, it is pretty easy to move with oars because it sits flat on the water—there is no keel hanging down to increase drag. Once safely outside the harbor, we hoisted the sail and got underway. We set the sail to run before the wind and started to pick up speed; air bubbles began to mark our trail across the dark green water.

It didn't take long to spot Heimaey emerging from the haze as we moved closer. We could see the steep sea cliffs that are teeming with seabirds. Soon we were right outside the entrance to the deep and well protected harbor. It was early afternoon when we arrived at the dock and secured the "Geirfálki." People at the dock told us that the cargo for Norway was ready to be loaded. This was the rest of Tryggve's smoked and dried fish, to be loaded on top of his previous cargo from Eyrar. I said, "After we finish the cargo and have everything secured, let us all go ashore except one man to stay on board in case of weather changes or any adjustment of lines may be quickly needed." The men usually work out among themselves who will be the one to stay with the ship.

So far "Geirfálki" has served us well; we have been to Horn, Reykjavik, Eyrar, and now we were at our last port, Heimaey in the Vestmannaeyjar Islands. We will spend a few days here before we set sail to return to Trondheim, Norway. I want to stay mainly to let the merchants here know about my ship and the cargo capacity it can handle, and also to get the word out that I have good experience sailing between Norway and Iceland. Before we sail I need to pick up one more good seaman from here for the return to Norway. I know they have very capable seamen in Heimaey, and since this is early spring, it should be easy to find someone.

Maybe in a few more years, when my brother Kaare has more experience, we might take off for that unknown land west of Greenland that Bjarni Herjolfsson discovered but didn't explore. But for now, I have to stop dreaming and tend to my responsibilities. That land west of Greenland will still be there, after I get "Geirfálki" safely back to Norway.

Historical notes for Part One

Latitude Sailing

There is historical evidence that latitude sailing was a favored   Viking method of sailing and that they used it extensively. Latitude sailing is mentioned in the Lanamabook (Book of the Landtaking) and the Graenlendinga saga. Given the lack of modern instruments and the locations of the destinations, latitude sailing was a most effective method. The Viking navigator would simply start the voyage from the latitude of the destination, and then sail straight across the ocean, directly west or east toward the desired goal. Using the tools and techniques described in this book, their headings were easy to maintain, except in severe weather.

The Vikings referred to the latitudes not by degrees but by the name of landmarks and places located at the corresponding latitude. For example, instead of saying lattitude 62° North, they used the name "Stad-Thorshavn" for the place from which they began the voyage (Stad, Norway), and their destination (Thorshavn, Faeroe Island) both located at 62° North. It is much like the naming convention of many early roads on land. I used the degree designation in this book so that the reader could better follow the routes.

Maritime Law

The evidence for maritime law in Viking times comes from two books of laws of early Iceland, *Gragas I* and *Gragas II*. Gragas means Gray Goose, a title of uncertain origin. This code, which is said to have been modeled in part on an older law, the Norwegian Gulathing Law, provided the basis for the Icelandic national assembly, which was founded in the year 930. It covers many aspects of daily life, including maritime issues. One point worth quoting is that covering the entry clearance for those entering Iceland. From the book *Gragas II*: *"Everyone is to pay a landing-place toll except men from Norway."*

The Tides and Docking in Port

The docks during Viking times were built very primitively, close to the shore for convenience, consisting of a few pilings driven into the mud with a plank deck on top. The tide was carefully considered when docking in port. At Reykjavik, for example, the tide is about 16 feet (5 meters). This variation in height required that the the the captains load and discharge cargo with the timing of the tide always in mind.

Cargo Commonly Carried

Many trips were made carrying "smoked and dried fish" which consisted of two types of preserved fish: codfish that was salted and then dried, and herring which was smoked. Timber was also a popular commodity, as was cloth and metal hardware and tools. Almost anything required for homesteading would find its way to Iceland and Greenland, while the resources of the new settlements would become the cargo for the return trip to Norway.

An Arrival Beacon for Horn, Iceland

The Vesturhorn mountain was the landmark the Vikings used when they approached Horn; in good weather, it was like a beacon it the sun. The mountain is 1886 feet (575 meters) high, and visible from about 46 nautical miles away from the deck of a *knarr*. There are two natural harbors, one on either side of the mountain, with good shelter and sandy beaches. This was one of the first settlements for early Icelanders, with the Vesturhorn mountain serving as a natural welcoming signal.

Viking Dress

Fewer examples of clothing for Viking men have been found than for Viking women. This is largely because many men of the Viking Age were cremated rather than buried.

Many textiles in the Viking Age were made of worsted wool in twill patterns. These wools were carefully woven, supple, attractively textured, and often dyed in bright colors. Areas, such as England, produced linen, which was imported and used. Silk was available all over the Viking world by the ninth century, and it was liberally used, much of the time for decorative purposes.

Vikings wore at least two types of trousers: a wide, knee-length, baggy type and a narrow, full-length, more fitted type. Over the torso was an undertunic or smock, usually of wool. Then came an overtunic of wool with metal clasps. There is also evidence that jackets or long coats were worn, decorated with elaborate metal trimmings. A cloak could also be worn for dress occasions. Cloaks included fancy embroidery with bright colors of stitching.

Most shoes were either half-boots or ankle shoes; some were slip-ons, some tied with leather lacing, and some used lappets with cylindrical leather buttons. Goatskin was often used for shoes, as was deerskin, calf, sheep, and cowhide.

A complete wool hood is most likely the head covering that would have been used at sea where protection from the elements is considered over style. The horned helmet, so often depicted as being Viking, is not supported by historical evidence.

Viking men were fond of personal ornaments. Thor's hammers, for instance, are found all over the Viking world. The remains of textiles and ornamentation recovered from the Viking age reveal a people who were much more concerned with style and fashion than most historians have depicted.

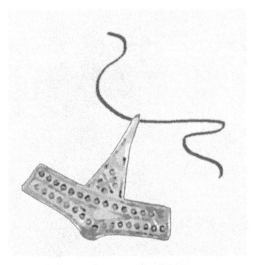

Cast of silver or bronze, Thor's hammer was
worn around the neck on a leather or woven string.

Western Settlement
Vesturbyggð

Ammassalik (navigation point)

Other Eastern Settlements:
　Bratahlid
　Gardar
　Herjolfsness

Eastern Settlement
Austurbyggð

Kap Farvel (navigation point)

Early Greenland Settlements and Navigation Points

Island of Unst: Shetland Islands
Major landmarks

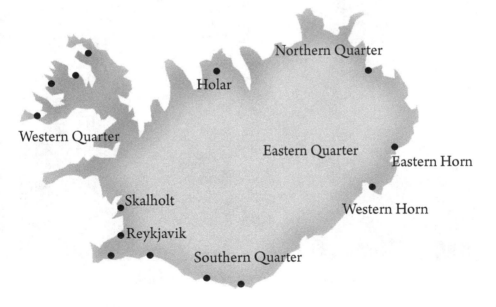

Some of the Early Settlements in Iceland

A replica Viking ship under sail off the coast of Iceland.

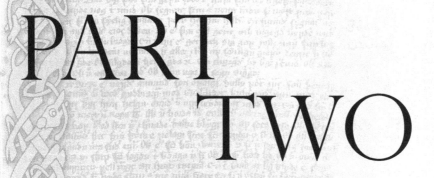

PART TWO

SHIPS, EQUIPMENT, AND NAVIGATION TECHNIQUES USED BY THE VIKINGS FOR OPEN OCEAN VOYAGES

*The majestic form of the Viking ship reflects the
underlying design of a practical sailing vessel.*

# CHAPTER TEN

The Viking Oceangoing Vessel

The vessel the Vikings used on their long voyages was the oceangoing 54 foot (16.5 meters) long *knarr*, with a beam of 15 feet (4.6 meters). The vessel was also known as the "Greenlands-knarr," since the ship was used on a steady and direct route between Norway and Greenland as a supply ship. The crew usually consisted of five to eight men. The ship could carry not only crew and cargo, but passengers, livestock and all necessary supplies. (*See Appendix 3 for a detailed comparison of the types of Viking ships.*)

Sailing times were traditionally measured in terms of days, one twenty-four hour day, from noon to noon, by using the sun's shadow for reference when the sun was in the south, LAN (Local Apparent Noon). The meridian observation of the sun was the most important navigational event of the day.

Speed

The average speed was around six knots; one average sailing day for the *knarr* was estimated to be 144 nautical miles (24hr x 6kn=144 nautical miles). Speed of the replicas has been determined by using GPS and modern methods; there is no reason not to think they closely approximate the original ships.

"Present experiments with Viking ship replicas show that with the wind 10-15 m/s (about 22-27 knots), the speed was 8 knots on a broad reach. When close-hauled the knarr sailed within 6 points (67.5 degrees) including drift. The drift was five degrees, and the speed was 6 knots. In 5 m/s wind (about 7-10 knots) the speed was 4.5 knots on a broad reach, and 3 knots when close-hauled."
                    —Vikingernes kølvan, Søren Vadstrup 1993

Lines of the rigging. They control the shape, height and position of the square sail used on Viking ships.

Rigging

A rope when used on a ship is usually called a line. These lines have many specific names such as the mooring line, which makes the ship fast to the dock. The halyard will hoist and lower the yard and sail. A sheet is used to trim the sail to the wind. The braces are lines used to square the yard (the horizontal timber which carries the sail). The sheets set the *hals*, and *skaut* (corners of the sail), and the bowline.

(*See diagram pages 10-11.*)

The sails that the Vikings used are called square sails, either rect-angular or trapezoidal shaped. In the Viking Age wool (*wadmal*) was the commonly used material for sails. This is known from accessible written sources. They used this mate-rial not only because it was readily available, but also because it is naturally waterproof due to its high lanolin content.

The head of the sail was lashed to a yard and the yard was secured to the mast by a *rakki* (*see illustration page 71*). The sail was hoisted manually by a halyard. The halyard was made fast at the middle of the yard, through a hole in the mast near the top, from there through a turning block, it continued down to a heavy crossbeam on the afterdeck where it was made fast to an extra strong belaying pin.

A square sail is set according to the wind and controlled with the braces. The braces are attached to the yard, one on each side of the yardarm. There are two more lines in the lower corners of the sail, which control the sail angle relative to the hull. The forward corner of the sail, called the *hals* (tack), is the most important and powerful part of a square sail.

Most of the drive is between the *hals* and the yard. The after corner of the sail is called the *skaut* (sheet). The bowline is attached to the forward vertical edge of the sail. It was made fast about a third of the way up from the foot (bottom) of the sail. It leads forward through a turning block at the bow of the ship. The bowline was used to keep the forward, vertical edge of the square sail tight when sailing close-hauled (as close to the direction of the wind as possible to sail). The bowline is double ended, so that on either port or starboard tack, the slack end leads to the opposite side of the sail, making it ready to become the hauling part when changing tack.

Priars are lines attached to the central portion (belly) of the sail running back to the mast like a horizontal vee, the point of the vee connecting with the mast at the bottom. The *priars* are very important on larger sails, such as the one used on the replica ship "Borgundknarren," *(discussed in the Appendix)* where the distance between the tack and the sheet is fairly long. Here there are three *belly priars*, at different heights, made fast to the sail. The top one goes from the sail around the mast back to a wooden block made fast to the sail, through the block and down to a cleat on the mast. The middle priar is made fast the same way. The bottom one is made fast at the foot of the sail, around the mast back to a wooden block made fast to the sail, through the block and back to a cleat at the mast. The *priars* are used to steady the foot of the sail and to adjust how deep the belly should be. They are also used to flatten the sail in strong wind.

It was mentioned in the sagas that the Vikings reefed the sails. In rough weather they could reduce the sail area by taking in one or more reefs. To reef the square sail, the sail was lowered and a section of the sail was secured by a band of reef points placed across the sail parallel with the foot of the sail. Then the sail was hoisted back up again.

The most advanced piece of sailing gear for its time was probably the removable pole called the *beitiás* (tack-pole). It was extended over the ships side. The *beitiás* was shifted from side to side, depending on the tack the ship was on.

Two heavy wooden blocks are secured to the ship's sides, both starboard and port. They are located between the mast and the bow. The wooden blocks on the *knarr* have three sockets, which allows the angle of the *beitiás* be adjusted for best performance of the sail. One end of the *beitiás* was inserted into the socket; the other end was secured to the *hals*.

The *beitiás* provided a great advantage, especially in heavy weather sailing. The *beitiás* transferred the tremendous energy from the *hals* to the ships hull. Recent experiments have proven that the *beitiás* improves performance on all courses except when sailing before the wind.

The beitiás *(tackpole) is shown laying across the rail. Note the three sockets, just above the deck, for inserting the end.*

The yard is the horizontal wooden beam that runs the width of the sail at the top and carries the weight of the sail.

The rakki *is the horseshoe shaped fixture used to secure the yard to the mast.*
The entire sail may be quickly lowered and easily raised.

Setting the Sail

When sailing close-hauled on a starboard tack:

The tack is made fast to the *beitiás* forward on the starboard side. The bowline is secured; the sheet and the port brace are made fast on the port side aft; the starboard brace is secured on the starboard side aft—but not tight, and the *priars* are then adjusted according to the wind. In rough weather this would have been a tough job since everything was done by hand.

When sailing close-hauled on a port tack:

The tack is made fast to the *beitiás* forward on the port side. The bowline is secured; the sheet and the starboard brace are made fast on the starboard side aft; the port brace is made fast on the port side aft—but not tight, and the *priars* are adjusted according to the wind.

When running before the wind (the wind coming from aft):

Both the sheets and the braces are made fast, leading aft. Both tacks are secured and leading forward. The *priars* are adjusted according to the wind.

The side rudder (steering oar) and tiller:

The side rudder is secured on the starboard quarter by a rope or thong through the upper planking and pivoted on a boss lower down, about halfway down, between the upper planking and the keel. The rudder is controlled by an athwartship tiller. On my two trips as a crewmember on the "Borgundknarren," I was very impressed by the way the side rudder performed. It is well balanced and easy to control.

The side rudder (steering oar) and tiller, showing attachment to the hull.

Viking Navigational Aids

The following navigational aids were probably used on all Viking voyages:

Sunstone

Horizon-board

Sun shadow-board

Lead *(dybdelodd)*

Stars

Current

Wind, swell

Birds, whales

Landmarks and seamarks

And most important: experience.

Most of these navigational tools, the sunstone, horizon board, sun shadow board and lead were discussed in the previous section.

Of these, the lead *(dybdelodd)* is probably the oldest of all navigational aids. It is a highly useful device, particularly in periods of reduced visibility near shore, leaving or entering a harbor, as the navigator must avoid running aground. The navigator simply throws the weighted end overboard and feels when it hits the bottom. From the markings on the line he then knows the depth of the water.

The tools and techniques used by the Viking navigators will also be discussed as we follow the voyages from the sagas in the next section.

The winds and waves are always on the side of the ablest navigators.

—Edward Gibbon

Adapted from a painting by the author: Approaching the Shore.

During the middle of the summer there is too much light in the night sky to see the stars at the high latitudes where the Vikings sailed. The sun was the only dependable celestial body available for reference.

# CHAPTER ELEVEN

Navigating by Sun and Crystal: The Sunstone

How did the Vikings manage to navigate across the open ocean for thousands of miles without conventional instruments? Many books have been written about their amazing voyages, but they don't offer much detail to explain their navigational methods. Furthermore, there are practically no navigational relics from Viking era sites to reveal any secrets; most suspected navigation tools found so far have deteriorated beyond recognition.

To fill in this missing part of Viking lore, we must try to imagine ourselves in that time—driven to explore what lies beyond the sunset, possessing great common sense and courage, but lacking any tools and techniques of modern navigators.

To begin with, based upon my experience as a modern navigator and on hints given in the sagas and in the old Icelandic lawbook, the Grágás, I firmly believe that the sunstone and some sort of a bearing board, similar to the horizon board described here, were used by the Viking navigators to guide them across the North Atlantic, and to the other destinations they reached. These simple but effective aids to navigation allowed the Vikings to claim their place as one of history's great seagoing people.

The Vikings mostly sailed in the middle of the summer, when the northern latitudes are experiencing long days and short nights. Consequently, the Vikings depended more on the sun than the stars for navigation. At the latitudes where the Vikings sailed, no place in the region experienced true darkness in the summer. At latitude 61 degrees north for example, from the end of April to the end of August the sun was available for more than 14 hours a day. At higher latitudes the sun was visible even longer. What more appropriate scheme could they have discovered to direct their ships than to use sunlight refracted through a crystal found on the ground in Iceland?

When the Vikings Used the Sólarsteinn (sunstone)

There were times during certain conditions, even in fog, that the sunstone could have been used at sunrise and sunset by the navigator. When very cold air moves over warmer water, wisps of visible water vapor may rise from the surface as the water "steams." In extreme cases this frost smoke, or Arctic sea smoke, may rise from a few feet to a height of several hundred feet. The portion near the surface forms a dense fog which obscures the horizon and surface objects, but usually leaves the sky relatively clear. Often in this type of fog, a ship passing by would have only the top of the mast showing with

This photograph shows surface fog—which could obscure the sun—with clear sky overhead, a common condition in summer in the North Atlantic.

the surface fog obscuring the rest of the ship. When the light from the rising or setting sun was lost in the fog bank, but the zenith was clear, the navigator could tell the exact position of the sun by using the sunstone, even though the sun itself was unseen.

Even on clear days, the horizon at sea is often obscured by haze or distant clouds. This was an ideal situation for using the sunstone to find the sun.

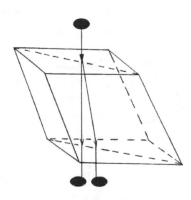

Light traveling through Iceland Spar is split into two rays resulting in a double image.

Historical Reference to Sunstones

Saint Olav's saga gives this explanation of sunstone: "A stone with which one could see where the sun was in Heaven." In one of the stories from the *Flateyjarbók*, King Olav the Stout (St. Olav) spent a couple of days with a farmer named Rødulf and his two sons, Dag and Sigurd. Sigurd told the king, "…even when I cannot see the heavenly bodies, I know the hour of the day and night…" The next morning the weather was overcast and snowing. The king remembered Sigurd's claim, and he requested Sigurd to tell him where the sun

This photograph clearly shows how one black dot appears as two when viewed through the sunstone.

was. Sigurd stated the exact position. Then the king held the sunstone in the air to see if Sigurd was right. The king confirmed the position of the sun with the stone.

In the sagas the exact type of stone remains a mystery, but the sunstone is associated with objects of high value and people in power. The sunstone is not only mentioned in the sagas it is also mentioned in the list of inventories from several Icelandic churches, but without details. The sunstone could have been an example of an item that the churches received as a tithe or church tax. One reference is from the *Sturlunga* saga:

> *"When Bishop Gudmund and Hrafn Sveinbjarnarson came back to Iceland, after having been one winter in Norway, Hrafn sailed west to Arnarfjord, to his farm in Eyri, now called Hrafnseyri. But before they parted, Bishop Gudmund gave Hrafn a good stud horse and [a] sunstone."*
> (McGrew translation)

The sunstone Bishop Gudmund gave to Hrafn Sveinbjarnarson must have been regarded as a treasure of high value since it came from the Bishop and it is associated with the good stud horse.

A few years ago I came across the book *Solstenen: Vikingernes Kompas* written by the late Danish archaeologist, Torkild Ramskou. In his book he mentioned four types of crystal that can work as a sunstone including andalusite, tourmaline, cordierite, and Iceland spar (also called optical calcite). I decided to experiment with Iceland spar, because the crystal was available to the Vikings in Iceland, and it shows double refraction better than any other crystal.

According to Dr. Sveinn Jakobsson of the Icelandic Institute of Natural History, Iceland spar is the only mineral candidate locally available in Iceland that would work as a sunstone. The other optical minerals are rather rare, and therefore it is unlikely they would have been used.

Iceland spar of good quality is mainly found in these localities in Iceland: Helgustadir in east Iceland, Akrar in west Iceland, and Djúpidalur in northwest Iceland. For a long time one of the best mines in the world for Iceland spar was at Helgustadir on the northern side of Reydarfjördur.

The Helgustadir mine was put under protection order as a natural monument in 1975 and it is strictly forbidden to remove anything from it. A vein of Iceland spar was also worked for a while near Hoffell in the Horn area where the Vikings landed. Due to Iceland spar's historic availability, the Vikings could have easily obtained the stone and exploited its natural properties. Imperfect (because of frost heave and weathering) Iceland spar crystals can still be found lying loose in the scree in some places.

Most of the specimens of Iceland spar in the museums outside of Iceland originated from this mine. In the days before synthetics, this mineral was also used for various types of scientific optical equipment such as microscope lenses.

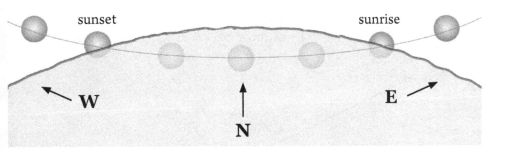

The sunstone readings are best at sunrise and sunset when the sun is just below the horizon, a condition that occurs all night in the Viking mid summer.

How Sunstones Work

Iceland spar is also known as optical calcite, calkspat, or silfurberg. It is composed of calcium carbonate. Optical calcite ($CaCO3$) has a rhombohedral crystal structure. Its opposite faces are parallel but there are no right angles. A perfect crystal is colorless and transparent. Optical calcite possesses the unique ability to split one ray of light into two rays of light, otherwise known as double refraction.

An object viewed through a crystal of Iceland spar will be seen as a double image. For example, make a small mark on a piece of paper and place the Iceland spar on top of the mark so that you are looking at the mark through the crystal. Two sharp and clear marks will appear side by side. Now, rotate the crystal while watching the marks. One mark remains stationary while the

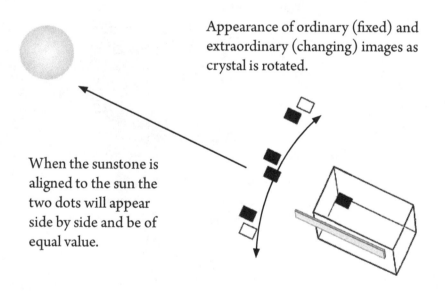

Appearance of ordinary (fixed) and extraordinary (changing) images as crystal is rotated.

When the sunstone is aligned to the sun the two dots will appear side by side and be of equal value.

A pointer stick placed along one of the longer sides aids in aligning with point on horizon.

other rotates around as you rotate the crystal. The stationary image is called the ordinary image and the rotating image is known as the extraordinary image.

In order to use a crystal as a sunstone for finding the sun, a small black dot is placed at the center of the top surface, so it will face up when the stone is held overhead. View this dot from underneath by looking up through the stone while holding it flat (level to the horizon). You will notice the single dot appears as two dots when viewed through the stone. Align the pointer you attached to a long side to the brightest area of the sky. Upon rotating the stone back and forth in the horizontal plane, you will see that one image fades and the other becomes darker. When the two images appear to be equal in value note the position of the stone and the pointer. The pointer will now be aligned to the true bearing of the sun. It is accurate to within one degree.

The basic principle of the sunstone is polarization of light, first observed by Erasmus Bartholimus in Copenhagen, Denmark in 1669. He also points out that when Iceland spar is covered with water, the surface loses its natural polish. When the surface of the crystal is slightly opaque, it can be made transparent again by coating the crystal with thin oil.

Christiaan Huygens in his *Treatise on Light* writes that he also studied the double refraction Bartholimus had discovered in the Iceland crystal. Both Bartholimus and Huygens made measurements of the crystal. Huygens mentioned there is a slight difference between Bartholimus observations and those which he made. Bartholimus, in his treatise of this crystal, puts at 101° the obtus angles of the faces. While Huygens puts them at 101°52', Bartholimus states he measured these angles directly on the crystal, which is difficult to do with ultimate exactitude because the edges are generally worn and not quite straight.

I have collected several pieces of Iceland spar crystals. My measurements consistently show: 101° 30' for the obtuse angle and 78° 30' for the acute angle. I used a protractor divided into 30' for measurements. The illustration on the next page will help the reader visualize the unique shape of the sunstone crystal.

Any Iceland spar crystal will work as a sunstone as long as it is optically clear. The thickness of the crystal is important. The thicker the crystal the better is the refraction (separation) of the black spots.

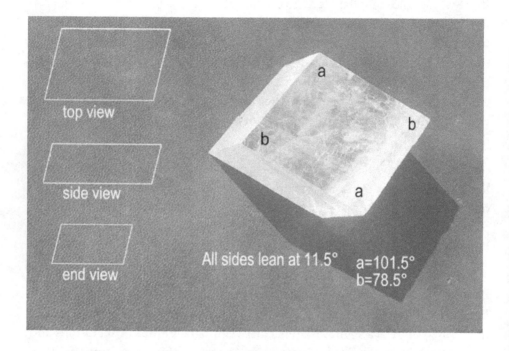

top view

side view

end view

a

b

b

a

All sides lean at 11.5° a=101.5°
b=78.5°

The shape of a sunstone is hard to visualize, and difficult to represent in a two-dimensional graphic. The sunstone has no right angles. Imagine a cube where every angle has been skewed away from the normal 90°; that is the configuration of a sunstone.

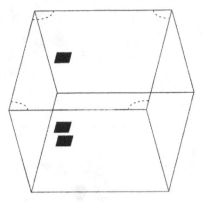

One dot on top becomes two dots when viewed from underneath looking up through the sunstone.

A Sunstone Summary

A sunstone indicates direction by means of the polarizing effect of the earth's atmosphere on sunlight. The strongest polarization arrives from a sky direction at right angles to the sun's direction. The Vikings could have discovered the sunstone's double image effect when looking at the sky through the crystal. A spot of dirt or a tarry fingerprint smeared on the crystal would have attracted their attention. The Viking navigator could have easily found and used the sunstone to indicate this phenomenon.

The readings are best at sunrise and sunset when the sun is slightly below the horizon. What the saga did not mention is the fact that although the sunstone will locate the hidden sun on an overcast day, a small clear patch of blue sky overhead is needed to insure a good reading.

The sagas suggest, and logic confirms, that the Vikings must have used the sunstones. Their use may have been kept as a closely-held navigational secret known only to qualified members of any crew on board. Therefore nothing was written down about how they were used at sea. Perhaps future excavation of Viking archaeological sites will find a sunstone and prove that they were indeed carried and used by the Viking navigators.

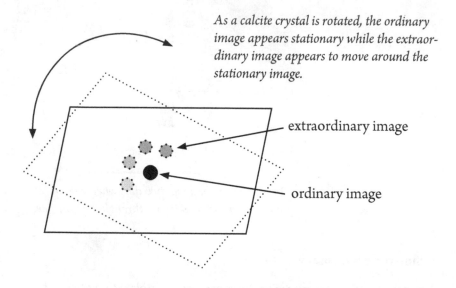

As a calcite crystal is rotated, the ordinary image appears stationary while the extraordinary image appears to move around the stationary image.

extraordinary image

ordinary image

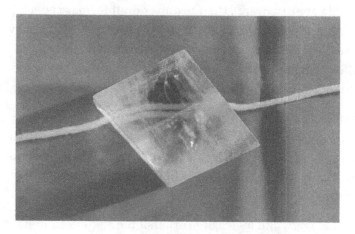

Transparent calcite crystal showing excellent rhomboidal cleavage and double refraction of the string beneath.

# chapter twelve

The *Áttir*, *Eykt* and the Horizon Board

The Vikings did not have a magnetic compass, but they had other ways to get their bearings and to guide the ships across the ocean. They divided the visible horizon into eight Old Norse sections, which they called *áttir*, meaning "main directions." They based this on the orientation of the Norwegian west coast, which runs approximately north and south. The use of *áttir* was a development of their navigation terms as they sailed coastwise and offshore to fish and work the sea, and eventually to voyage to distant lands.

The sections were named:

Nordr (N)

Landnordr (NE)

Austr (E)

Landsudr (SE)

Sudr (S)

Utsudr (SW)

Vestr (W)

Utnordr (NW)

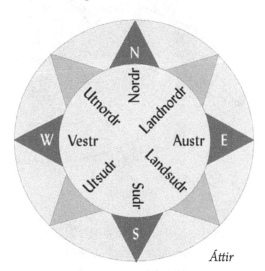

Áttir

Later on when they settled the islands to the west, these names for the directions went with them; they are still in use today in those places such as the Faeroe Islands, and in Iceland.

Without a compass the Vikings reckoned directions using *áttir*.

A Specific *Áttir* Direction Defines a Reference for Time: *Eykt*

An Old Icelandic law book the Grágás (Gray Goose) explains the bearings of the sun, and the definition of *eykt*, an afternoon position of the sun used for directional reference and timekeeping.

Eykt is the time when, if the southwest eighth of the sky is divided into three, the sun has passed through two parts and has one part still to pass.

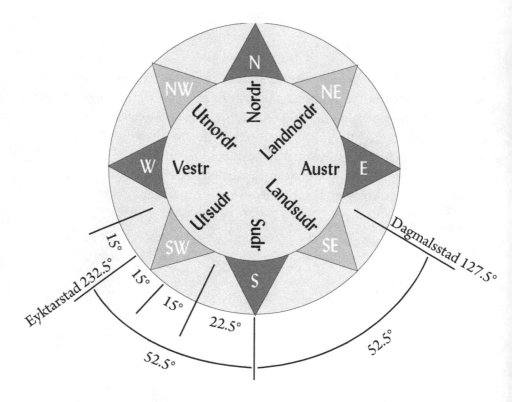

From the *Grágás I*, Page 41. *"Latin nonae (originally 1500 hours) and eykt seems to have come to define about the same time: 1500 to 1530 hours."* From the Islandic dictionary: *eykt: a time of three hours; dagmál; the time about nine o'clock AM.*

Thus it was that the Vikings used a direction to reckon time as well; that is, when the sun was located at *eykt* the hour was three to three-thirty.

86

The apparent motion of the sun is westward around the earth, from sunrise to sunset, at a constant speed of 15° of longitude each hour (360°/24hr = 15°/hr). This motion can be translated into a bearing change along the horizon when the height of the noon sun is low, which is the case when viewed from high latitudes. In this case, it takes the sun 3 hours and 30 minutes to travel from noon (bearing 180°) to *eyktarstad* (bearing 232.5°).

> Bearing change = 232.5° - 180° = 52.5°
> Time change = 52.5°/15 = 3hrs 30m
>
> *Eykt* = 3hr 30m after noon = 15:30 Local time.
> Dagmal = 3hr 30m before noon = 08:30 Local time

The position of the sun in the *áttirs* also allowed simple time references to be made without a clock. "Now the sun is just past *eykt*arstad" references a time that any Viking would understand.

These terms, *eyktarstad (eykt)* and *dagmalsstad (dagmals)*, refer to a direction that leads to the horizon, what is today termed a bearing. Using the *áttirs* to reference true bearing, the Vikings could keep the ship on course. The direction was always a true direction without any local magnetic variation or magnetic disturbance.

(See Appendix 6 for Viking concepts of the 24-hour day.)

Mechanics of the Horizon Board

To demonstrate how the Vikings used the horizon board to get their bearings, I have created my own horizon board. This is not a replica of an artifact, but an original device based upon information from the previously mentioned Old Icelandic lawbook, *Grágás,* and the configuration of the old Norse horizon.

The horizon board is simply a flat surface, such as a flat board, upon which is recorded the *áttir.* Also indicated are the azimuths of sunrise and sunset over the sailing season, on certain latitude. The horizon board shows how this information about the sun and the eight sections of the horizon could be put to use in navigation.

The Vikings referred to latitude not by degrees but by the name of landmarks and places located at the appropriate latitude. For example: Instead of saying latitude 62° North, they used the name Stad, Norway, the place they sailed from, and the name of their destination, Thorshavn, Faeroe.

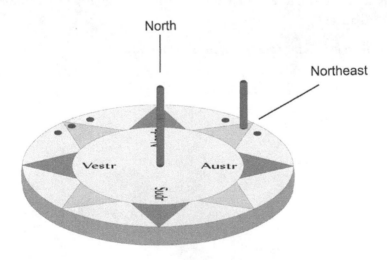

*Horizon board set up for 61° North showing
the direction of the rising sun on May 21.*

The horizon board shows how a Viking navigator could, with observations he had made at home, sail a latitude course from a homeport, across the ocean to his family's homestead, as recorded in the sagas.

Use of the horizon board also allows the navigator to make good use of the sunstone to find his course amidst a dense fog or clouds obscuring the horizon. Such basic navigational tools, or ones very much like them, would have been needed.

The horizon board on page 91 visually demonstrates the direction of the rising and setting sun during the months of May, June, and July, on the 21st of each month at a given latitude. Small holes on the edge of the horizon board are used with wooden pegs to mark the direction to the sun. Notice during the months of May, June, and July at 61° north, the narrow variation of the sun's bearing at sunrise (or sunset) is 010°: May 21st, 045°, to June 21st, 035° and back to 045° on July 21st. The navigator had a close check on his course, even if he assumed the sun's bearing didn't change from May through July.

Horizon board bearing alignment is achieved with the use of a sunstone when the fog is on the horizon at sunrise.

89

The horizon board is quite easy to use. For example: assume the navigator desires to set a course due west *(vestr)* from his departure point at Hernar Norway (61° north) on May 21st on a clear morning. The sun will rise here at 045°, northeast *(landnordr)*. The wooden pegs on the horizon board will be set in the appropriate holes on the horizon board, and a true bearing of the sun will be taken. With an accurate reference bearing, the desired course west can be read from the horizon board.

The same procedure is used for all other months. But if clouds or fog hides the sun, as often the case in these waters, then the sunstone will be needed.

At sunrise on a morning with an obscured horizon and a clear zenith, the sunstone can be set up to find the exact bearing of the sun. When this is done, the horizon board will be aligned with the sunstone's bearing to the sun at 045°. The horizon board shows the sun's true bearing and the desired course can then be determined from it.

A horizon board for other latitudes is easily made. The principle is the same except that the bearings are different.

During the frequent foggy conditions, the use of the sunstone with the horizon board was a good combination, as the information obtained is truly valuable to the navigator. Knowing the location of the sun, he can align the horizon board and determine other directions hence and the heading of the ship.

Using the horizon board and the sunstone a Viking could, with observations he made before leaving, sail a latitude course from a homeport, across the ocean to his family's homestead, and back again, as written about in the sagas.

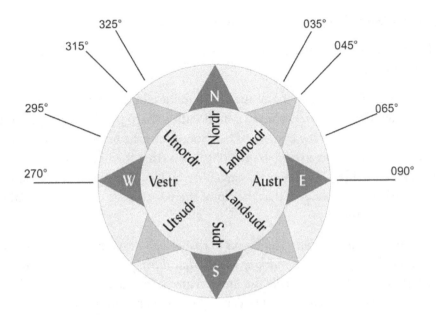

**Horizon board for 61° North showing the direction of the rising
and setting sun for different dates of the year in modern times.**

Sunrise		Sunset
035°	June 21	325°
045°	May/July 21	315°
065°	April/August 21	295°
090°	March/September 21	270°

Sumer Solstice (*Sommersolhverv*)   June 21-22

Equinox (*Jevndøgn*)   March 20-21   September 22-23

Winter Solstice (*Vintersolhverv*)   December 21-22

> *A individual horizon board is must be fashioned for each latitude of
> sailing. This is not too much of a challenge for the Viking navigator,
> since they sailed relatively few latitudes.*

Using a "Sun Shadow Board" to Stay on Course

The reader can construct and test this navigation aid by following these instructions:

Obtain a flat wood board about 8 x 10 inches. In the center, drill a hole to receive an upright dowel or small pencil with a sharp tip. This upright should be at a right angle to the board and the board must be level. Now the board should be located on a stable bench or table so that it will not be disturbed, in a place outside, where the Sun can shine on it during a full day. We are going to track the shadow that the tip of the pencil casts on the horizontal board during the day.

When the early morning sun begins to cast a shadow on the board, mark the tip of the shadow; continue marking the shadow during the day at one hour intervals. With these marks you will also have created a sun dial, telling the local time for the season. After sunset, draw a curve through all the marks, and you have the curve of the sun's path for that particular day, but in practice also for some days ahead.

Where the curve is closest to the center, the shadow is shortest, and the sun has its highest altitude. Here the shadow is pointing north or south, depending on your geographical latitude and the season. From this north-south line, you can create the compass points or degrees, and now you have a true sun-compass.

To use the compass, place yourself in the sun and hold the compass level. Then turn it until the point of the shadow is exactly on the curve, in mornings over the western half and in afternoons over the eastern half. This is how the compass is showing true directions.

(Adapted from *Viking Navigation*—Søren Thirslund)

If you board a vessel and head out to sea, you now need to align the vessel with the board. Once underway, steer so as to keep the shadow made by the tip of the pencil aligned with the arc previously inscribed on the board before you left home. If you can keep the alignment throughout the day you will be "sailing the latitude" and your heading will be true.

The sun's true bearing in summer for northern latitudes

60º North	Sunrise Bearing	Sunset Bearing
May	047º	313º
June	037º	323º
July	047º	313º
August	065º	295º
61º North	**Sunrise Bearing**	**Sunset Bearing**
May	045º	315º
June	035º	325º
July	045º	315º
August	065º	295º
62º North	**Sunrise Bearing**	**Sunset Bearing**
May	043º	317º
June	032º	328º
July	043º	317º
August	064º	296º
64º North	**Sunrise Bearing**	**Sunset Bearing**
May	039º	321º
June	025º	335º
July	037º	323º
August	062º	298º

This table shows the bearing of sunrise and sunset, on the 21st day of the summer months, for four primary latitudes at which the Vikings sailed.

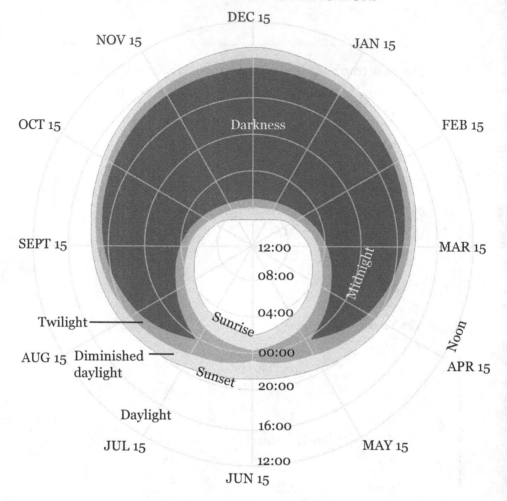

The "Circle of Day and Night" for the year 1000 at latitude 61° North. The hours of the days and nights are plotted around the year. Notice that from May 15 to July 15 there is no darkness at all.

To a navigator, "twilight" begins when the brightest stars become visible: "darkness" is when the horizon is no longer discernible.

Based on our present calendar, in the year 1000 the longest day was June 15th.

CHAPTER THIRTEEN

Finding True North by the Sun

The Vikings had the sun's shadow to find true north each day at noon. The basis for this method is simple. Compare the length of an afternoon shadow with that of the morning shadow.

> "Though we can use the sun for direction, without proper instruments it is usually impossible to measure the height of the noon sun, the problem was not only the sun's height but also the brightness."
> —David Burch, 1990

> "A distinctive method of determining the meridian is by a variation of the equal altitude method."
> —Bowditch, NGA Pub. 9, 1962

With this in mind, we can imagine how the Vikings could have used the shadow pin method. This way they did not have to look up in the sky at all, but instead kept track of the shadow, and avoided going blind.

At the time of the meridian passage the sun is highest and the shadow is shortest. In northerly latitudes, this will be when the sun is in the south and the shadow is pointing

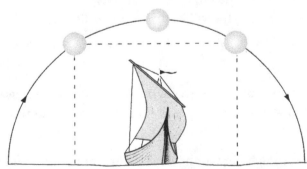

Sighting the sun before and after noon at even offsets from noon.

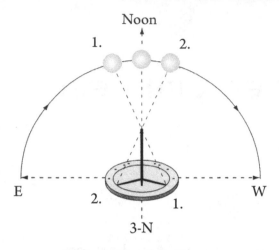

Finding true north by the sun
1: Before noon
2: After noon
3: Noon
(looking south)

true north. Do not depend on finding the true north by measuring the shortest shadow because around noon the shadow stays about the same length while its direction changes rapidly.

Some time before noon the navigator sets up a steady course. A cloud on the horizon or a landmark will work for the duration of the observation.

When marking the location of the shadow, the heading must be the same for the two readings; the one before noon and the one in the afternoon. A shadow pin is placed with the sharp point up, perpendicular to the horizon, in the center of a flat board level with the horizon.

The navigator marks the first point where the tip of the pin's shadow falls and draws a circle through this point with the base of the pin at its center. A string from the base of the shadow pin to the first mark could have been used for this. In the afternoon, when the shadow again touches the circle, he marks his second point. Midway between the two points lies the meridian of the observer. This will be the north-south line.

> *"The shadow pin method is the best way to get direction from the sun."*
> —David Burch, 1990

As the sun moves westward, shadow moves eastward. Near midday all shadow tips move due east, regardless of your location or the time of the year. We can find an east-west line from shadow motion.

A straight line connecting the first and the second mark will run west to east. The second mark will be east of the first one.

From their meridian observation, when the sun was in the south, the Vikings were able to get a north-south line. At the same time a west-east line was also obtained.

The navigator could have taken an observation and plotted his course before leaving port, then maintained his east-west direction by making an observation at midday each day during the voyage (weather permitting). Keeping track of a shadow tip motion at sea is not as easy as on land, but it can be done if the weather is calm enough, or if some type of gimbal is used to keep the board level with the horizon regardless of the ship's motion.

An historical reference where the Vikings used the sun for navigation is in the *Grænlendinga* saga, in the story about the young captain Bjarni Herjolfsson. Bjarni arrived in Iceland at Eyrar with his ship in the summer of 985 or 986. That same year his father, Herjolf Bardarson, had just left Iceland with Eirik the Red and several hundred other settlers to colonize Greenland.

This news of his father's leaving came as a shock to Bjarni. His crew asked him what he was going to do next; he answered that he was thinking of sticking to his old habit of staying with his father in the winter. "I will sail to Greenland if you will come with me," he explained. They all said they would go with him whatever he did. Bjarni said, "I suppose it will be a foolish voyage on our part, as none of us has been on the Greenland Sea." But all the same they put out to sea as soon as they could, and sailed for three days, until the land sank into the sea. But the fair wind dropped, and there was north wind and fog, and they did not know were they were going.

Day after day passed like this. Then the sun came out again, and they were able to get their bearing from the sky. This had to be at sunrise, noon or sunset. Knowing the true direction to the sun at these times, a true reference bearing, they could reestablish their course. A bearing taken at any other time was meaningless to the Norse navigator due to lack of a reference point. We have to remember they didn't have a magnetic compass.

After the bearing was established and a new course set, they hoisted sail and continued the voyage, eventually becoming the first Europeans to sight the coast of North America.

How Wind and Current Affect the Ship

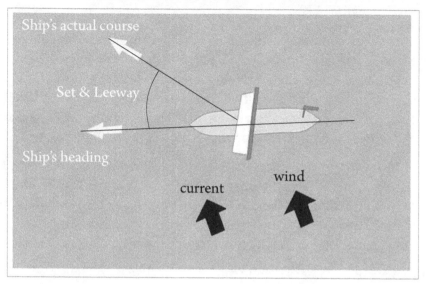

Current moves the ship off course in the direction of the current. At sea, current tends to align with the prevailing wind. Wind moves the ship off course in the downwind direction.

"Set" is the difference, due to current, between the ship's heading (the course steered) and the course actually sailed.

"Leeway" is the difference, due to wind, between the ship's heading (the course steered) and the course actually sailed.

Wind, current and swell all act upon the ship to influence the direction the ship actually moves through the water.

Wind direction is always described as the direction from which it blows. A northerly wind is a wind blowing from the north toward the south.

Likewise, the direction of swells means the direction from which the swells are coming.

Unlike the wind and swell direction, the current direction is always described as the direction *towards* which it is flowing. A westerly current is a current running toward the west.

CHAPTER FOURTEEN

Steering by Wind and Swell

Steering by the wind and swell means holding a steady course using wind and swell directions as reference. The sun was used to find the wind and swell directions at sunrise, noon, and at sunset. Direction of wind means the direction from which the wind is blowing. For example, July 21st at latitude 61° N on a clear morning, the sun will rise at NE (045°). The horizon board is set at NE (045°)—this will be the true bearing to the sun.

On the horizon board there is a pin in the center of the board. If a cloth ribbon is attached to the top of the pin, the navigator could then read the wind direction from the horizon board. At noon he could get an up-date by using the shadow pin method to find true north first, then check the wind direction to steer by.

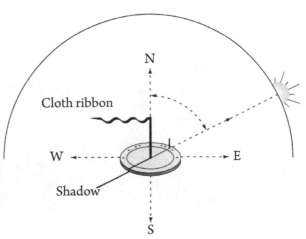

The horizon board is used to first find sunrise bearing, then the wind and swell direction may be determined and used as reference to steer by.

At sunset the navigator used the same method as used in the morning. The true bearing of the sunset, 315°NW, would then be used to set the direction to steer by.

The more often the direction of the wind and swell is verified, the more accurate the course becomes. Once on course, a reference mark on the horizon near dead ahead can be used. At night this could be a star; during the day it could be a slow moving cloud formation on the horizon. A long pennant on top of the mast, which can be seen from the steering position, could also have been used to maintain the course.

Direction of swells means the direction from which the swells are moving. Swells are waves that have traveled beyond the wind systems or storms that have generated them, or waves that persist after the generating storm has died away. Swells are more regular and stable in their direction than waves. Sometime swells can be felt better than they can be seen, having flattened out after travelling long distances.

The navigator oriented his ship to the swells according to the ship's heading. For example, the swells coming at an angle will cause the ship to yaw. If the motion changes, the navigator knows that the ship is no longer on the

Swells causing the ship to yaw.

correct course (assuming the swells remain constant). Then the navigator must reorient the ship to get the motion right again. When the seas become choppy and confused, navigation by ocean swells becomes more difficult or impossible.

Detecting the Direction of Ocean Swells

Swells coming at an angle will cause the ship to yaw; swells coming from the side will cause a rolling motion; swells from the bow will cause a pitching motion. These motions can be felt in the movement of the ship and heading adjustments may be made accordingly.

Swells causing the ship to pitch.

Swells causing the ship to roll.

A Note on Swells and Women Navigators

Visually detecting the direction of a prevailing swell and using that information for a heading reference is difficult when the swell is partially masked by the presence of wind waves or interference if there is more than one swell pattern present at the time. When one swell is not prominent visually, the "feel" of the boat motion is often an accurate way to detect the swell. Boat motion, even in a complex seaway, is often repetitive, and the passing of a swell crest can be a clear marker within the pattern. Once the pattern is detected, changes in the frequency or magnitude of the disturbance is a measure of the heading relative to the swell.

Ancient and even relatively modern Polynesian navigators have used swell patterns extensively as steering guides in lieu of conventional compass and other aids. Famous among them for this perception was the woman navigator Paintapu (around 1780 in the Gilbert Islands). Her method was to lay on the floor of a vessel for hours, guiding and judging when to tack by viewing stars overhead and feeling the motion of the boat under her, while lying on her back. *(See Lewis, 1994.)*

The role of women navigators in Viking times has not been documented, but there is no reason to doubt that they took part. Some of the most famous clipper ships racing around Cape Horn during the Gold Rush days were guided by women navigators. *(See Shaw, 2001.)*

Despite the more popular myths that have survived, that women bring bad luck on a vessel and so forth, the more we learn about true maritime history, the more we can appreciate the role they played.

CHAPTER FIFTEEN

Star Navigation

Polaris the "North Star"

The northernmost star is Polaris, the "North Star." It is known that the Vikings used Polaris for navigation as they named it "Leiðarstjarna" the "guiding star."

Around year 1000, in the midst of the Viking age, Polaris was about 6° from the true celestial pole of rotation. For Polaris to be precisely over the North Pole, the declination of Polaris would have been N90° exactly, but the declination was only N83° 46', which was 06° 14' off the pole.

The Vikings would notice that Polaris remained close to one point in the northern sky and use it for their north direction, by which they navigated by holding Polaris at a fixed point. To find Polaris, they used the Big Dipper Configuration. Dubhe and Merak, two stars on the cup end of the Big Dipper, point to Polaris. With these two stars, called the pointers, the navigator drew an imaginary line between them and

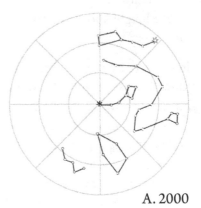

A. 2000

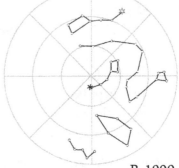

B. 1000

Spring positions of stars near Polaris at same hour for the years: 2000 and 1000, as viewed from Oslo, Norway.

extended the line to Polaris. The distance to Polaris is five times the distance between the pointing stars. When clouds obscured the Big Dipper, however, the Vikings could locate Polaris as the last star on the handle of the Little Dipper.

Determining Latitude by Polaris, the "North Star"

Latitude is distance in degrees north or south of the earth's equator. One degree of latitude equals 60 nautical miles. In modern times, Polaris lies due north at a height above the horizon approximately equal to the latitude of the observer.

In the high northern latitudes, Polaris is high in the sky. At 61° north latitude, Polaris is about 61° above the horizon. At 50° north latitude, Polaris is about 50° above the horizon, etc.

"First use of the pole star to determine latitude is not known, but many centuries ago seamen who used it as a guide by which to steer were known to comment upon its change of altitude as they sailed north or south."
—Bowditch, NGA Pub. 9, 1962

Polaris descends toward the horizon as your latitude decreases. The North Star is the only star that essentially does not move, always bearing due north.

To sail north the Vikings kept Polaris at a fixed point on the bow. To sail any other direction they could hold Polaris at a fixed point on the beam, stern, or any points between. To sail west they kept Polaris on the starboard beam. Even when Polaris was 6° off true north, the navigator could used the orientation of the Little Dipper to assist in finding true north. *(See Appendix 9.)*

Steering by Polaris with the aid of the horizon board would have taken the Vikings to their destination. Polaris is as bright as the stars of the Big Dipper (Ursa Major).

While the Vikings sailed primarily in summer, many voyages were of necessity still made in the spring and autumn, when the stars were still visible in the high north. Bjarni Herjolfsson could have taken advantage of the North Star on his voyage from the coast of the North American continent to Herjolfsness, Greenland in the autumn of 985 or 986. Steering by the stars was common knowledge in navigation.

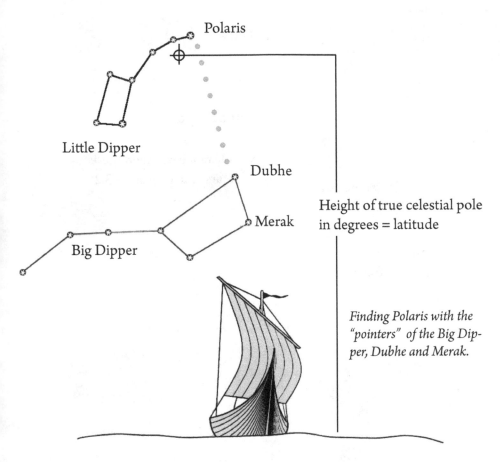

Height of true celestial pole in degrees = latitude

Finding Polaris with the "pointers" of the Big Dipper, Dubhe and Merak.

When sailing west, the direction of the bow was held towards a low star on the western sky, and the line to Polaris was kept on the starboard beam.

Star directions change as the stars move across the sky. From time to time it was necessary to shift to another star to steer by, again using Polaris for orientation. Northern stars always rise north of due east and set north of due west.

Just by knowing the altitude of Polaris at his home port, the navigator could, by observation, tell if he was set north or south of the intended route. Higher altitude meant he was set farther north, lower meant farther south. A measuring reference for this observations could have been made by turning the bow directly north and, while standing at the stern, marking the height of Polaris against the mast.

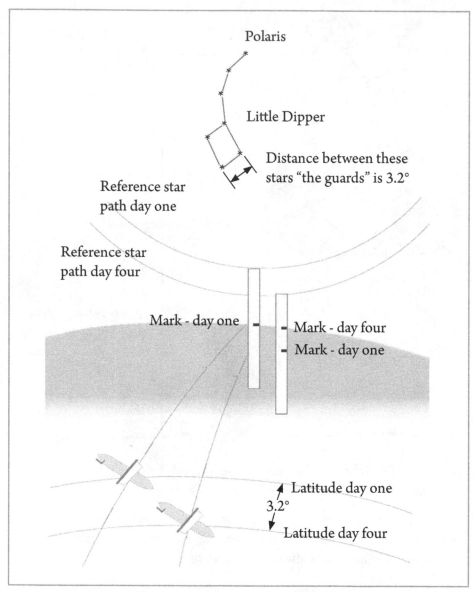

Polaris

Little Dipper

Distance between these stars "the guards" is 3.2°

Reference star path day one

Reference star path day four

Mark - day one

Mark - day four

Mark - day one

Latitude day one

3.2°

Latitude day four

Simple Viking method for determining distance north or south of desired latitude: hold a small piece of wood or horn at arm's length and mark the position of a circumpolar reference star above the horizon, at twilight on consecutive days. The position of the marks will show if the course has been set north or south. In this example the ship is heading eastward and has been set south by about 3.2°—the distance between "the guards" (stars of the Little Dipper)—by day four. This 3.2° distance could have been used to judge how far off course the ship actually was, although the Vikings would not have used these terms to describe the process.

A Viking Secret for Reckoning Distance Off Course Using the Circumpolar Stars

Now we know enough about the movement of the stars around Polaris to imagine how a Viking navigator would prepare for a voyage with these stars in mind. Knowing the altitude of Polaris could be helpful, but stars closer to the horizon are much easier to note and mark on a reference board when at sea. The stars that circle about the celestial north pole every twenty-four hours without setting are called circumpolar stars. These are the ones that would be most helpful from the moving deck of a ship. Circumpolar stars are visible all night long, every night of the year, but they would be most useful for navigation as they passed near the horizon on their arc below the pole as they headed eastward. At a fixed latitude, a given circumpolar star always passes the same distance above the horizon at its lowest point (directly below the pole) and this distance can be easily measured to monitor latitude.

The Arabs are known to have used a device for referencing star heights for navigation; the device is called a kamal.

—David Burch, 1990

Before leaving home in Norway, he would have measured and marked the position of all useful circumpolar stars that he could use for reference. If our navigator lived in the northern part of the country, he would need to board his ship and sail down the coast to the latitude that corresponded with the latitude of his destination. He would prepare a reference marker that would give the distance from the horizon to the useful circumpolar stars at his new sailing latitude; this mark he would use for reference during the voyage while "sailing the latitude" directly west.

For easiest measurement, a star would need to have an altitude below 20° or so, and would need to be clearly visible in the northern sky, near the horizon, during twilight. There are several candidates for bright stars that skimmed the northern horizon in Viking times during twilight—recalling that northern twilight can last for a very long time at high latitudes.

Calculated for the year 1000 at 61° North, some bright stars that skimmed the horizon include these:

Capella is an ideal reference star, crossing the northern meridian at 15° high in the spring.

In March the crossing is at 4:00 am, in April at 2:00 am, and in May at midnight. There is enough darkness in all cases to get a good reading.

In June and July, no stars are visible near the horizon, the summer sky being too bright.

In August and September, the star Alkaid crosses the northern meridian at 25° a couple of hours after midnight.

In October, Vega becomes a possible reference star, crossing at 9° some 4 hours after midnight.

The navigator's "secret" would be how to find the right star and choose the correct time to measure. He might also measure many times and take the lowest value to make the result more accurate. *(See Appendix 9.)*

Calculations for star positions in the year 1000 were made using the StarPilot electronic calculator (www.starpilotllc.com) from Starpath School of Navigation, Seattle.

Zenith Stars

The point in the sky directly overhead is called zenith. A star that passes directly overhead has a declination (in degrees) equal to the latitude of the observer.

The Vikings surely noticed that at specific latitudes certain stars passed directly overhead. This is especially easy to observe on land. It is probable that the Vikings used zenith stars for navigation at sea as well. It is known that other cultures, the Polynesians for one, navigated by zenith stars.

In the Viking age, around the year 1000, in the latitude where the Vikings sailed, there were four prominent stars that could have been used as zenith stars: Megrez, Merak, Alioth, and Mizar, all located in the Big Dipper Configuration. The declination of the these four stars were Megrez N62° 34', Merak N61° 37', Alioth N61° 30', and Mizar N60° 18'. Megrez is the fourth star in from the handle, Merak is one of the pointers, Alioth is the third star in from the handle and Mizar is the second star counting from the end of the handle, between Alkaid and Alioth.

"...the Polynesians, are known to have used zenith stars, they used the brightest stars to guide them over thousands of miles of open waters and back."
—Kyselka & Lanterman, 1976

The zenith star for Ålesund, Norway, was Megrez. The latitude for Ålesund is 62° 28'N. Two of the stars, Merak and Alioth were the zenith stars for Ytterøyane at latitude 61° 34'N, Florø at latitude 61° 36'N, and Kvanhovden at latitude 61° 42'N. The same two stars, Merak and Alioth also passed directly overhead on the Faeroe Island of Suduroy (Syderø).

The star Mizar could have been used to guide the ships on a voyage between Lerwick, Shetland, and Marstein area in the entrance to Bergen, Norway, in latitude 60° 10' N and 60° 08'N respectively. An observer's zenith star passes directly over him once every twenty-four hours. The zenith stars would have been most useful to the navigator in the spring and early autumn, when it was still completely dark and the stars were brightly visible. For a rough estimate, they could have used the mast as a sighting device to determine when the star was at zenith, or at least the highest point when sailing east or west.

If we examine the declination (the star's latitude) of the four zenith stars that were indicated in the Big Dipper for the latitudes the Vikings sailed, and for some of the places the Vikings settled, you will see a correspondence. This may not have been just a coincidence. If Vikings used the zenith stars for guidance, just as the Polynesians did, they would have established routes, and destinations directly corresponding to the latitude they were sailing. On land, before departure and after landfall, it is not at all difficult to determine fairly precise latitudes by zenith passage.

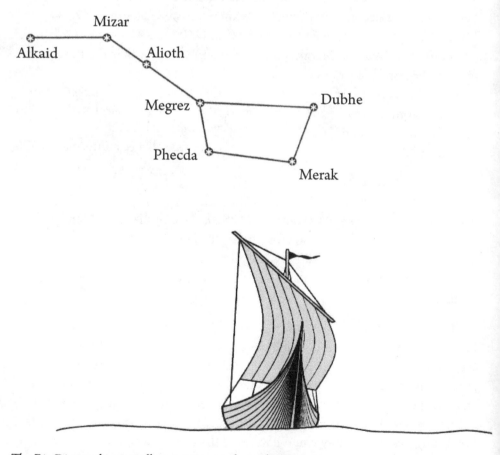

The Big Dipper showing all major stars and zenith stars (Merak, Megrez, Alioth, and Mizar) that were used as guides.

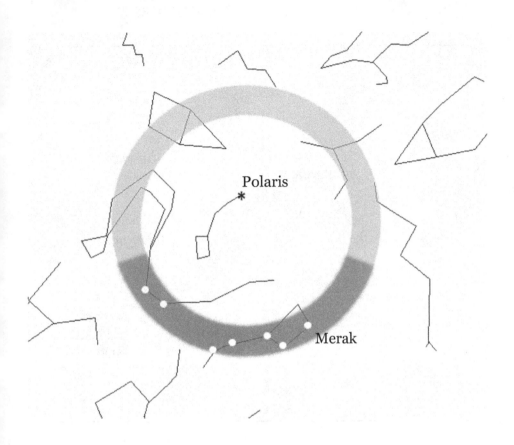

The circular band above represents the sky overhead on March 15, 1000, for latitudes 59º N to 65º N. Zenith stars are shown in the darker section (night). In other months different stars in the gray band would pass overhead during darkness.

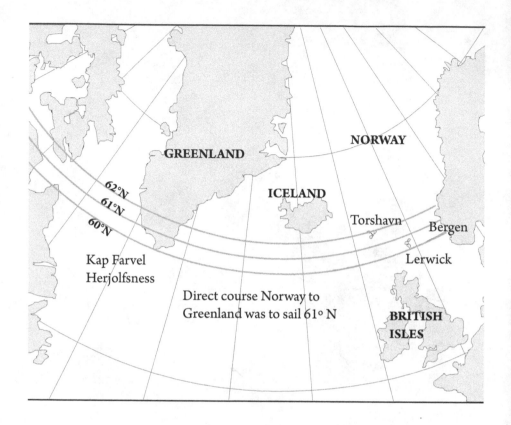

60° N Guide Star: Mizar

Guides the ship between Bergen, Norway and Lerwick, Shetland, and further on to Kap Farvel and Herjolfsness—the Eastern Settlements of Greenland.

61° N Guide Stars: Merak and Alioth

Guides the ship between western Norway (Florø) and Suduroy, Faeroe, and the direct course from Hernar, Norway to Greenland.

62° N Guide Star: Megrez

Guides the ship between Stad, Norway and Torshavn, Faeroe, and the between Ålesund, Norway and Torshavn, Faeroe.

The Declination Change for Certain Northern Stars			
Star	Year 1000	Year 2000	Change
Polaris	N83° 46'	N89° 17'	N 5° 31'
Kochab	N78° 12'	N74° 10'	N 4° 02'
Dubhe	N66° 56'	N61° 44'	N 5° 12'
Merak*	N61° 37'	N56° 24'	N 5° 13'
Megrez*	N62° 34'	N57° 02'	N 5° 32'
Phecda	N59° 13'	N53° 43'	N 5° 30'
Alioth*	N61° 30'	N55° 59'	N 5° 31'
Mizar*	N60° 18'	N54° 57'	N 5° 21'
Alkaid	N54° 30'	N49° 20'	N 5° 10'

*Zenith star

Considering the four zenith stars of the Big Dipper, there is a correspondence between the stars latitudes, the routes the Vikings sailed, and the places they settled. This points to the probability that the zenith stars were used as primary guides in establishing their latitude sailing routes.

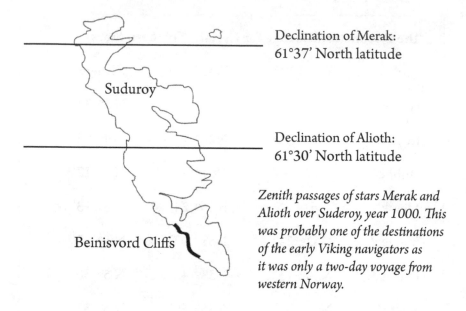

Declination of Merak:
61°37' North latitude

Declination of Alioth:
61°30' North latitude

Zenith passages of stars Merak and Alioth over Suderoy, year 1000. This was probably one of the destinations of the early Viking navigators as it was only a two-day voyage from western Norway.

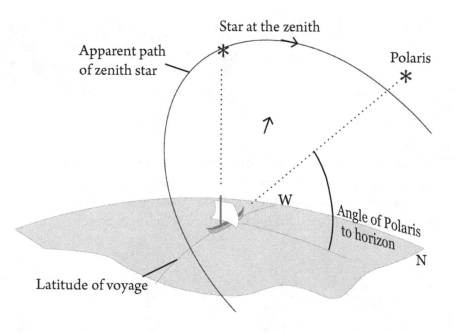

Zenith star for a given latitude, in the season of visibility, will pass overhead during the night and may be used for latitude reference.

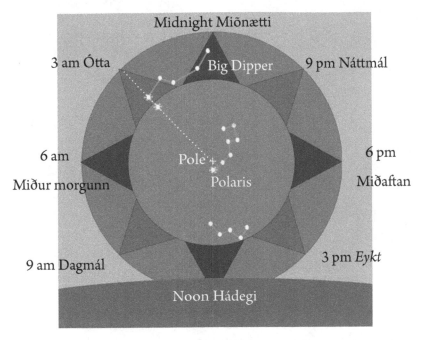

A "skyclock" based on the Big Dipper. The time is centered in Ótta, about 3 am. Note that the sky is a mirror image of the áttir.

Viking Nighttime "Skyclock"

To tell time from the Big Dipper, as one example of a generalized star clock, imagine its pointers as the end of line whose pivot point is the celestial pole, and imagine the 24-hour clock face printed backwards on the sky as shown above. The Vikings would have read the time in the terms of their *áttir*, but would have had to imagine its mirror image, as the stars sweep counterclockwise.

In this example, midnight is straight up from Polaris; 0600 hours is to the west of Polaris and 1800 hours to the east. When the pointer stars point straight up from the horizon, the clock reads midnight; when the hands point east with the pointers lying parallel to the horizon the clock reads 1800, and so forth.

All star clocks are fast; they gain 4 minutes each day or a whole day in one year. Since the voyages only lasted a few weeks at most, star positions were a useful reference if they "set" the clock by noting the relative position before leaving on a trip.

Statue of Leif Eiriksson at Shilshole Bay Marina, Seattle

PART THREE

VOYAGES OF THE VIKINGS
ACROSS THE NORTH ATLANTIC
AS DESCRIBED IN THE SAGAS...
FROM THE NAVIGATOR'S
POINT OF VIEW.

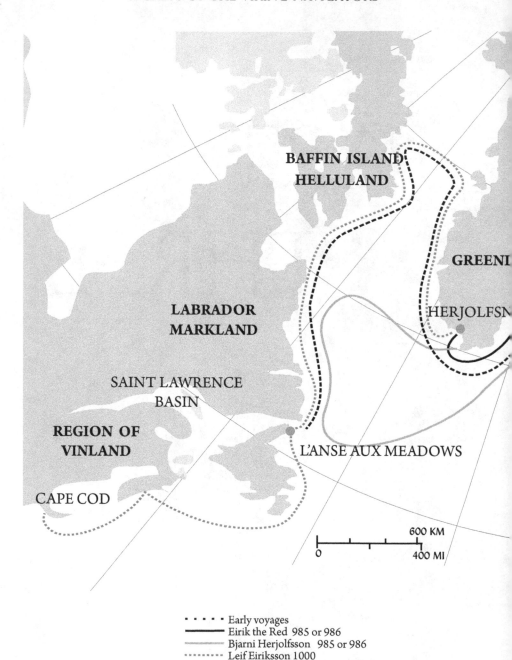

BAFFIN ISLAND
HELLULAND

GREENI

LABRADOR
MARKLAND

HERJOLFSN

SAINT LAWRENCE
BASIN

REGION OF
VINLAND

L'ANSE AUX MEADOWS

CAPE COD

600 KM

0   400 MI

· · · · · Early voyages
———— Eirik the Red 985 or 986
———— Bjarni Herjolfsson 985 or 986
·········· Leif Eiriksson 1000
- - - - - Thorfinn Karlsefni 1005

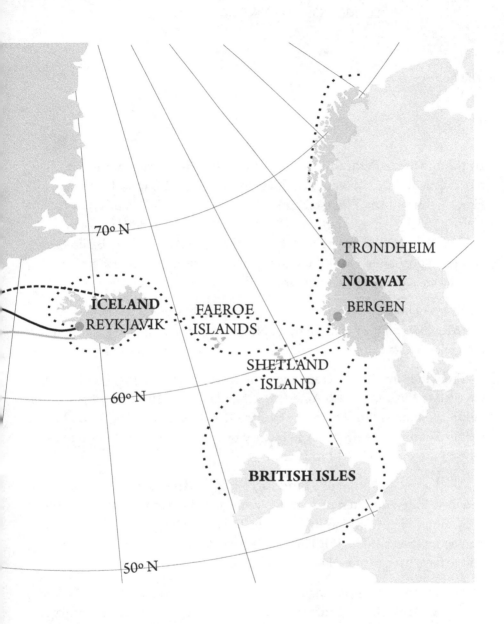

Map of the Viking Voyages

The Sagas

By the end of the fourteenth century, the main sailing directions for the North Atlantic area were written down in the Icelandic sagas. Both Bjarni Herjolfsson and Leif Eiriksson are said to have found three lands they named Helluland (slab-land), Markland (forest-land), and Vinland (land of grape-vines). Helluland and Markland were probably the present day Baffin Island and Labrador, while Vinland was somewhere between the St. Lawrence Bay and the area of Cape Cod to the south.

Ruins of houses and other Norse remains have been discovered at L'anse aux Meadows on the northern tip of Newfoundland, by a Norwegian author Dr. Helge Ingstad and his archaeologist wife Anne Stine Ingstad.

From the *Grænlendinga* saga and *Eiriks* saga we are told that Leif Eiriksson voyaged to Vinland (North America) around the year 1000, about 500 years before Columbus. The end of the westward exploration had been reached. Leif Eiriksson earned his place in history by being the first European to set foot on the shore of North America.

The Icelander, Þorfinnur (Thorfinn) Karlsefni, tried to settle Vinland, but had to abandon the attempt after two years due to the stiff resistance of the indigenous people. Returning home to Iceland, he settled at the farm Glaumbær in Skagafjörður. With him were his wife Guðríður, and son Snorri, said to have been the first European child born in North America.

Several notations of sailing instructions are preserved in the *Landnámabók* (Book of the Landtaking), first compiled in the twelfth century, which describes the settlement of Iceland. The translation varies from book to book, but the subject in each is consistent.

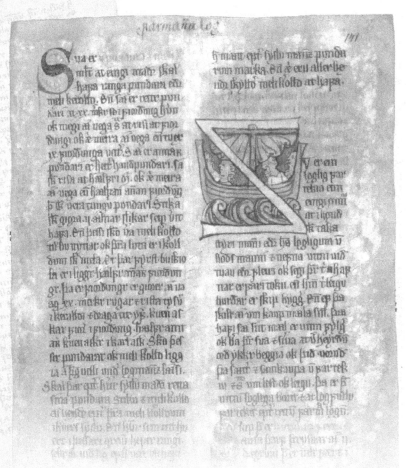

One statement goes as follows:

Svá segja vitrir menn, at ór Noregi frá Staði sé sjau dægra sigling í vestr til Horns á Íslandi austanverðu; enn frá Snæfellsnesi, Þar er skemst er, er fjogurra dægra haf í vestur til Grænlands. Enn svá er sagt, ef siglt er ór Björgyn rétt í vestr til Hvarfsins á Grænlandi, at þá mun siglt vera tylft fyrir sunnan Ísland. Af Hernum í Noregi skal sigla jamnnan í vestur til Hvarfs á Grænlandi, ok er þá siglt fyrir norðan Hjaltland svá, at því at eins sé þat, at altgóð sé sjóvar sýn; enn fyrir sunnan Færeyjar svá, at sjór er í miðjum hlíðum, enn fyrir sunnan Ísland, at þeir hafa af fugl ok hval. (Translation next page.)

121

The translation reads:

According to learned men, it is seven days sail from Stad in Norway to Horn in the east of Iceland; and from Snaefellsnes (on the West Coast of Iceland) it is four days sail to Hvarf (near Kap Farvel) in Greenland. From Hernar in Norway to sail a direct course to Hvarf in Greenland, you pass so far north of Shetland that you sight land in clear weather only, then so much south of the Faeroes that half the mountains are in the water, then so much south of Iceland that you will see whales and birds from there.

These instructions are a summary of the many voyages the Vikings had by then completed. They had apparently been successfully following the known routes for several hundred years. As we have pointed out, the evidence in the sagas confirm that latitude sailing was the preferred sailing method, and the routes sailed share commonly followed latitudes.

In this section we will follow several of the saga voyages, examining the navigation techniques the Vikings employed and the latitudes they sailed.

CHAPTER SIXTEEN

Following Routes Described in the Sagas

Before any voyage took place, the navigator had to prepare his ship, take on supplies, review the route, and make sure his navigation aids were carefully selected. Then he waited for favorable weather. He had to chose the best condition to set sail—when the wind and weather were most favorable— not only for the voyage at sea but also for leaving the shore. When going on a long voyage it was better to wait a few days to catch the right wind and weather. The sagas often mention that they were "waiting for fair wind" (*lå og ventet på bør*) to start a voyage.

For the navigator to reach his destination he needed to keep track of his reference course, guide the ship to the general vicinity, locate land in that area and use known landmarks for orientation. Some landmarks were high snow covered mountains on Greenland and Iceland, and volcanoes on Iceland. The reference course represents the ideal course the ship would sail, given perfect wind, current, and weather conditions. To keep to the reference course the navigator used his navigation aids.

Since most of the long sea voyages were generally in an easterly or westerly direction, it became common practice to first sail to the latitude of the destination along the coast, and then follow this parallel until landfall was made. For latitude they used common places such as Stad, Hernar, Horn, Snæfellsjökull, Vatnajökull, Kap Farvel, etc.

123

Stad, Norway to Thorshavn, Faeroe, and Horn, Iceland

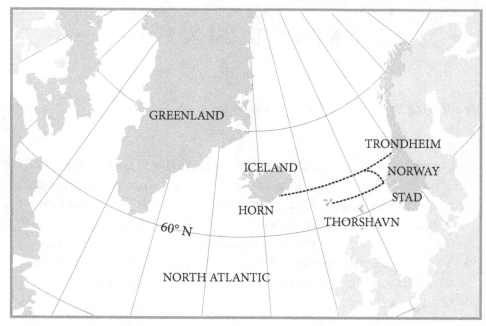

Sailing by Latitude:
Stad, Norway to Thorshavn, Faeroe at 62° North
Stad, Norway to Horn, Iceland at 64° North
Trondheim, Norway to Horn, Iceland at 64° North

For an ideal voyage the following criteria will be used:

Distance: approximately 660 nautical miles (Stad-Horn)
Distance: approximately 332 nautical miles (Stad-Thorshavn).
Reference course: west.
Weather: variable.
Speed: average 6 knots.
Latitude sailing: sailing at approximately 62º and 64º N
Time: June, July, and August (best months for voyaging).

Primary Mountain Peaks of Iceland:
These snow-covered mountain peaks were used like beacons of white light by the Viking navigators as they approached land.

Bárdarbunga

+ Vatnajökull glacier

+

+ Öraefajökull

Snaefellsjökull

Eyjafjallajökull

+ +

Myrdalsjökull

When the Vikings left Stad, Norway for either Thorshavn, Faeroe or Horn, Iceland, (reference point Kråkenes, 62°02'N, 04° 54.3'E) they left from one of the most dangerous places on the Norwegian coast, the Statthavet area. It has long been known as an area with very severe weather, and many have identified the area as dangerous.

"The depths vary between approximately 60 and 150 meters. It is indicated that winds, especially from the southwest to north create rough seas. In those circumstances the waves come straight in from the ocean. The current in the waterway has been estimated at between two and four knots and when the ocean waves meet it, strong steep waves develop and the swell becomes choppy."
(Quote: Den Norske Los, 1990.)

125

Even though it was dangerous in bad weather, they must have chosen this place because it was at the correct latitude. When there was a fair wind, the Stad area was the perfect place to set sail from.

When on a voyage to Thorshavn, Faeroe, the Vikings headed straight west on latitude 62° North until the destination was reached; the course was adjusted for current and leeway. The latitude of Thorshavn is 62° North. The distance from Stad to Thorshavn is about 332 nautical miles.

Note the bird perched at the top of this wind-sculpted floating ice.

When the Vikings sailed from Stad, Norway for Horn on the southeast coast of Iceland, they sailed north for approximately one day, or about 120 nautical miles to latitude 64° North. Once they reached the latitude of their destination, 64° North, they turned west. When on course they sailed at constant latitude until they saw the landmarks on Iceland. The Vikings used the ice cap Vatnajökull, for a landmark. The Vatnajökull is located on the southeast coast of Iceland. It is one of the world's largest ice caps, comparable to those of Antarctica and Greenland.

On the Vatnajökull is Mount Oræfajökull with a height of 6,952 feet (2,119 meters) which can be seen just on the horizon from some 86 nautical miles away. After Oræfajökull was sighted dead ahead, they kept their course west until they saw another mountain, the Snæfell. If the ship was on course, the Snæfell, with a height of 4,343 feet (1,324 meters) could have been seen about 70 nautical miles away on the starboard bow. The navigator then changed course to steer straight for the mountain of Snæfell until they saw the entrance to Horn, reference point Stokksnes (Vesturhorn) 64°14'N, 14° 58'W. If the weather and wind permitted, they sailed straight into the harbor.

Total distance from Kråkenes, Norway to Stokksnes, Iceland is approximately 660 nautical miles, including 120 nautical miles latitude change from latitude 62° North to latitude 64° North at the beginning of the voyage.

Trondheim, Norway was another major port in the Iceland trade. The voyages to and from Iceland were usually made in the summer months, but voyages where also made in the spring and autumn, weather permitting.

After departure from Trondheim, the Vikings sailed out the Trondheimsfjord. Once they cleared the coastal area and reached the latitude of their destination, 64° North, they changed course to due west following roughly the 64th parallel until landfall on the southeast coast of Iceland was made, using the Vatnajökull for a landmark. The destination was Horn in the Hornafjördur area.

Ships sailing clockwise around the coast had the advantage of the coastal current which flows in a clockwise direction around Iceland. The tidal current also moves in a clockwise direction around the coast. The tidal range is largest on the southwest coast and decreases on the north and east coast.

There is no good shelter along the coast between Höfn and Vestmannaeyjar. In bad weather this part of the coast can be very dangerous due to a current flowing towards the coast. At the time of the sagas the Vikings gave this section of the coast a very wide berth to avoid being shipwrecked.

When they approached an unknown coast or harbor after dark, it was best to stay well off shore and delay the arrival until daylight. Entering a harbor with a *rå* sail (square sail) required both courage and seamanship.

"If he comes back here when he has been away for three winters, he is as free from penalty as if outlawry had never befallen him."

—From the laws of early Iceland *Grágás* lawbook

We of course have no way of knowing what Eirik the Red really looked like, but this Viking reenactment player must be close.

CHAPTER SEVENTEEN

Eirik the Red's Voyages Between Iceland and Greenland

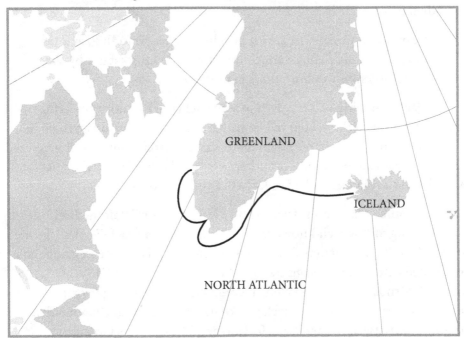

GREENLAND

ICELAND

NORTH ATLANTIC

Route map of first trip of Eirik the Red.

For an ideal voyage the following criteria will be used:

Distance: approximately 770 nautical miles.
Reference course: west, then coastal around southern Greenland.
Weather: variable.
Speed: average 6 knots.
Latitude sailing: sailing at approximately 65° North until landfall.
Time: June, July, and August (best months for voyaging).

According to the sagas, there was a man named Thorvald Asvaldsson who came from Jæren near Stavanger, Norway. He had a son named Eirik Thorvaldsson, later known as Eirik the Red, who was born about the year 950, the same year Bjarni Herjolfsson was born in Iceland.

Eirik was about thirteen years old when his parents had to leave Norway because of a feud that ended in homicide. They sailed to Iceland. They settled first at Drangar on the coast of Hornstrandir, because by this time most of the good land in Iceland was taken. Eirik's father, Thorvald Asvaldsson, died there.

Later on when Eirik was a grown man he married Thjodhild and left Drangar for Haukadal, a place which was later called Eirikstadir by Vatnshorn. Leif Eiriksson was born there in the year 971.

In Haukadal, Eirik was involved in a quarrel with his more powerful neighbors and was driven out of Haukadal. He took refuge on an island in the entrance to Hvamsfjord. Again there was a quarrel. This time it was was followed by a sentence of lesser outlawry, by the *Þorsnesþing* (Thorsnes Assembly). As a result, Eirik had to leave the country for three years.

With some of his closest friends and a fair wind, Eirik left the Breidafjord area heading for the well-known landmark, the glacier Snæfellsjökull, located on the 62-mile-long peninsula called Snæfellsnes. It is one of Iceland's most renowned landmarks. The glacier Snæfellsjökull caps the 4,743 feet (1,146 meters) dormant volcano Snæfell. It could have been seen approximately 72 nautical miles away from the deck of a *knarr*. It was used as a landmark on the voyages between Snæfellsnes Iceland and Herjolfsness Greenland.

Taking departure at Snæfellsnes, Eirik headed due west across the ocean following roughly the 65th parallel until he made his landfall on the East coast of Greenland near the Midjökull (the Middle Glacier) " ... *in the region of Ammassalik area, where they spotted the 11,000 foot pinnacle of Mount Forel trusting its peak up through the ice of Kronprins Fredriks Glacier to form a great black patch which shows up sharply against the gleaming inland behind it.*" (Mowat, 1965.)

The Vikings named the peak Blåserk (Blueshirt) from the way it looked. When Blåserk was sighted, they turned southwest to take advantage of the wind and the east Greenland current. The east Greenland current flows in

A crew used caution when approaching an unknown shoreline, even in calm seas.

a southwesterly direction. The wind during the sailing season was mostly from the northeast.

After the course change, coastwise navigation was used for the rest of the voyage. They followed the current and used the high mountain peaks for landmarks, until they rounded the Hvarf area (now called Kap Farvel), where Eirik sailed in to a place, that later on was called the Austurbyggð (the Eastern settlement).

Eirik used his three years in exile to explore this new country he discovered, which he called Greenland, because he said that people would like to go there if the land had a good name. After three years in Greenland, Eirik was free to return to Iceland. He sailed back to Iceland reversing the course for the Snæfellsjökull, and brought his ship and friends safely back into Breidafjord.

Soon after Eirik's return, difficulties with his troublesome neighbors started up again. Eirik decided that this was the time to leave Iceland for good. That was Eirik's last winter in Iceland. The following summer Eirik the Red left Iceland to settle in Greenland. He set sail for Greenland in the summer of 985 or 986.

Twenty-five ships with several hundred prospective settlers sailed from Breidafjord and Borgafjord in Iceland, but only 14 ships reached there; some were driven back, and some were lost at sea.

Just imagine what it must have been like onboard the *knarr*; an open sailing ship on a voyage from Iceland to Greenland. The ship was crowded with personal belongings, tools, livestock, and families. The weather was rough; the ship was constantly taking water over the railing. Everyone was taking turns bailing to keep the water out and to keep the ship from sinking. They were soaked to the skin from rain and continuous spray from seawater. To make matters worse, they wore inadequate and unwashed clothing; there was no place to get dry and clean up. The fresh water supply onboard was strictly for cooking and drinking. This was the condition of the people on the voyage when Eirik the Red set out to colonize Greenland.

After arriving in Greenland, most of the settlers established themselves in the Eastern Settlement (Austurbyggð). There were three communities: Brattahlid, Gardar, and Herjolfsness. Brattahlid was Eirik the Red's farm, a place he set aside for himself and his family. Eirik the Red and his wife stayed at Brattahlid. They had three sons: Thorstein, Thorwald, and the well-known Leifur Eiriksson (better known as Leif). Eirik the Red commanded great respect, and all the people in Greenland recognized his authority.

Brattahlid is now called Qassiarsuk in Eiriksfjord. Gardar (Igaliku) is located in the Igalikufjord. Gardar became the episcopal seat of Norse Greenland in the early 12th century.

Herjolfsness (Ikigait) which lies across the fjord from Fredriksdal (Narsaq Kujalleq), was one of the most important Norse settlements in the Eastern Settlement (Austurbyggð). It was a regular port of call for the Greenland *knarr* ships. The rest of the colonists sailed farther up on the west coast of Greenland and created the Western Settlement (Vesturbyggð), in the Ameralikfjord area, which the Vikings called Lysefjord. This fjord is located just south of the present day capital of Greenland, Nuuk (Godthåb).

CHAPTER EIGHTEEN

Direct Route from Snæfellsnes, Iceland to Herjolfsness, Greenland

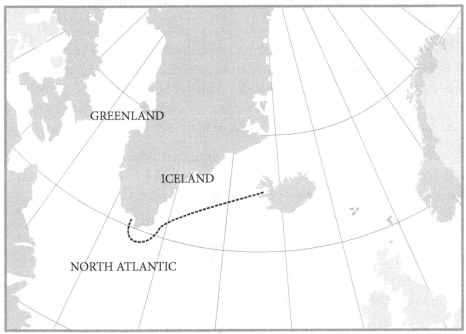

The direct route from Snæfellsnes, Iceland to Herjolfsness, Greenland.

For an ideal voyage the following criteria will be used:

Distance: approximately 675 nautical miles direct route.
Reference course: west-southwest until mountains are sighted, then coast-wise around southern Greenland.
Weather: variable.
Speed: average 6 knots.
Time: June, July, and August (best months for voyaging).

Unlike Iceland, where the climate has been influenced by immense thermal activity and has remained stable, the climate of Greenland has varied over the centuries. When Greenland was first colonized in the tenth century its climate was warmer than it is today. The sagas do not mention ice as a navigational hazard in Greenland waters until the late thirteenth century. In the fourteenth century the Vikings were forced to abandon the old sailing route from Snæfellsnes, Iceland to the Ammassalik area in Greenland, because of the increased hazard to navigation by pack ice in the area due to change in the climate.

From then on the Vikings sailed in a more direct route from Snæfellsnes to Herjolfsness. They continued using the Snæfellsnes as a landmark, which they could see approximately 72 nautical miles out to sea from the ship's deck. By this time the sailing routes were well established, and the Vikings were familiar with the weather and current in the North Atlantic ocean.

Leaving Iceland for Greenland, the navigator set a course in the *utsudr áttir*, meaning they sailed in the southwest section. After about twelve hours sailing, the Snæfellsjökull disappeared below the horizon.

At the beginning of the voyage they had to deal with the Irminger current that curves toward the north and northwest to join up with the east Greenland current southwest of Iceland. The east Greenland current flows in a southwesterly direction. The direction in which a current flows is called its set; the speed of the current is called drift.

With the current and the wind on the starboard quarter, the ship was set to port and the navigator had to compensate for the set by heading up to starboard. Otherwise they could have missed Kap Farvel entirely just like Bjarni Herjolfsson did in the late part of summer of 985 or 986 A.D., when he and his crew, driven off course by the current and north wind, were lost in fog for days on their voyage from Iceland to Greenland.

With the course adjusted, they headed in a direction between *vestr* and *utsudr* (west-southwest) until the high mountain peaks on the southeast coast of Greenland were sighted, especially the 8,238 foot high mountain west of the Danell fjord, and Paatusoq, about 30 nautical miles inland. In very clear weather, the mountain could have been seen from about 95 nautical miles away from the deck of a *knarr*.

After landfall they turned southwest to follow the coastline and stayed with the east Greenland current. Coastal navigation was used for the rest of the voyage using known landmarks to guide the ship to its destination. The distance from Snæfellsnes to Herjolfsness is about 675 nautical miles on the direct route.

In the late part of spring or early summer they were not able to sail too close to the coast of Greenland due to pack ice. The cold East Greenland current carried pack ice, together with icebergs, south to Kap Farvel and around to the west coast following the current. Sea ice varies from season to season.

At times it must have been difficult to get into the settlements due to the ice in the area. Today the fjord area around Quqortoq (Julianhåp) requires cautious navigation due to the present pack ice that often stays until late summer, particularly around Kap Farvel area.

This photograph shows what must have been a common sight in early spring: icebergs.

The original route the Vikings first sailed from Snæfellsnes, Iceland to Herjolfsness, Greenland is about 770 nautical miles. The settlement of Greenland was not the end of their westward exploration. There was a great deal of talk about searching for the land Bjarni Herjolfsson had seen further west from Greenland.

Much of the southern coast of Iceland is too rugged for landing a Viking ship—or any ship for that matter. Another skill required by the Viking navigator was the ability to land the ship safely once the destination was in sight. In some places, a perilous shoreline made completing the voyage as much of a challenge as enduring it.

CHAPTER NINETEEN

Hernar, Norway to Ikigait (Herjolfsness), Greenland

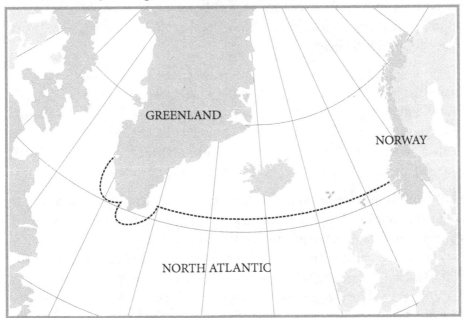

Route from Hernar, Norway to Ikigait (Herjolfsness), Austurbyggð, and Vesturbyggð, Greenland.

For an ideal voyage the following criteria will be used:

Distance: approximately 1,500 nautical miles.
Reference course: west.
Weather: variable.
Speed: average 6 knots.
Latitude sailing: sailing at approximately 61° North.
Time: June, July, and August (best months for voyaging).

After leaving Hernar, Norway, approximately 25 nautical miles northwest of Bergen in the Hjeltefjorden, the course was set due west. Hjeltefjorden extends about 26 nautical miles in a northwesterly direction from Hjelteskjer Light to Fedje, and forms with Herdlefjorden and Byfjorden the northerly approach to Bergen.

Approximately thirty hours later, after landmarks in Norway disappeared below the horizon, Shetland would have been sighted on the port side. With the Norwegian coastal current on the port beam, the ship would have been set to the right (starboard) which allows the ship to clear the northern tip of Shetland, at Muckle Flugga.

The first landmark they saw would have been the two hills on the north side of the island Unst. The Saxa Vord (two nautical miles west of Holms of Skaw), a pyramid-shaped hill, that rises steeply from the coast with a height of 932 feet (284 meters), would have been seen just on the horizon about 35 nautical miles away. The other hill, the Hermaness Hill, with a height of 653 feet (199 meters), would have been sighted on the horizon shortly thereafter.

When the ship was abeam of Hermaness Hill, they would see another landmark, Muckle Flugga Island. Muckle Flugga (60° 51'N, 00° 53'W) was very important. Although not the largest of a group of rocky islets and rocks extending north from Herma Ness (northwest corner of Hermaness Hill), Muckle Flugga might have been one of the most important landmarks the Vikings used for navigation—a stepping-stone to the Faeroes, Iceland, Greenland, farther on to Labrador, and then on to the East Coast of America.

The distance from Hernar, Norway to abeam Muckle Flugga, Shetland is about 165 nautical miles. When the ship was abeam Muckle Flugga, they were about ten nautical miles off the island.

Once again they put the land astern and continued west until Suderoy (Syderö), the southernmost island of the Faeroes, was sighted on the starboard bow. The point Akraberg (61° 24'N, 06° 40'W), where the navigator could check his course, is on the south end of the island of Suderoy. With the North Atlantic current on the port bow, the ship was set closer to shore.

This was something they had to adjust for, and they also had to beware of the strong tidal current in the area near shore.

The Vikings may also have used the Beinisvörd (Bejnesvör) cliffs and a mountain three nautical miles northwest of Akraberg Point on Suduroy (Syderö) as a landmark. The mountain is 1,506 feet (459 meters) high. Both the mountain and the cliffs could have been seen about 42 nautical miles at sea. From the saga: "...half the mountains are in the water." (See Appendix 7.)

The distance from Muckle Flugga, Shetland to abeam Beinisvörd Ciffs on Suderoy, is about 170 nautical miles, or about 30 hours sailing depending on the current and wind condition. Suderoy Island was the last visible landmark until the Vikings would see the high mountains on the southeast coast of Greenland.

With Beinisvörd Cliffs astern and the course adjusted to west, the navigator was now looking for seamarks, namely whales and birds, approximately 140 nautical miles south of Iceland.

According to the Landnámabók, "... they sailed so much south of Iceland that you will see whales and birds." It is also mentioned that "... they sailed so far south of Iceland that land was out of sight."

The coastline between Höfn and Vestmannaeyjar is very dangerous. There is a current flowing towards the coast and in bad weather the tidal current is irregular and strong. The tidal current could be very violent, especially when the wind was against it. The same goes for all the islands in the North Atlantic. It was best not to sail too close to shore.

When sailing on the leeward side of an island or close to cliffs, very strong gusts of wind and down drafts from high land are frequent. Extreme care was necessary to avoid being smashed up against the rocks. This was one of the reasons that the Vikings sailed about 140 nautical miles south of Iceland when on a direct voyage between Norway and Greenland.

This was one of the feeding grounds for the baleen whales, as well as fish and huge populations of seabirds, which feast on the seasonally abundant food supply. The Vikings would have seen the whales when they crossed the Reykjanes Ridge area on their way to and from Greenland. While the whales were busy eating krill, the seabirds were picking up food for their chicks.

According to Aevar Petersen of the Icelandic Institute of Natural History, in many seabird families, both parents go out every day to forage for the chicks, often making several trips a day. Some of the species are: gannets, auks (which includes the murres), gulls, cormorants, fulmars, puffins. All these birds travel out to sea for various distances from their colony to feed. The distance they may be seen off shore depends on the species and location of feeding grounds (which may shift).

Most activity from a sea bird colony takes place in the early morning hours. The fulmars normally go farthest and they may stay away from their nest and chicks for days, roaming the open seas hundreds of miles from their colony on such trips. Most of the other species make several trips to and from the colony every 24 hours, and they generally don't go out as far as the fulmars.

The murres can travel 50 to 100 nautical miles from the colony; the puffins travel about 75 nautical miles. The puffins, murres, kittiwakes, and the gannets are especially noted for travelling in small flocks back and forth from the feeding grounds. The diurnal flights of these birds were useful signs for the navigator. Observing the daily flight patterns of seabirds can indicate the direction of islands which were out of sight range.

The seas around and the coastal waters of Iceland remain one of the richest fishing grounds in the world. There is also an abundant marine mammal population including several species of whales.

The Orkneys, Shetlands, Faeroes, and Iceland are all extremely important breeding grounds for over 20 different seabird species in the North Atlantic region. It is well known among people inhabiting these islands that the sight of seabirds at sea during the summer indicated land was near. These were undoubtedly important clues for the navigator. The same technique using bird flight patterns would have been used when approaching Greenland. If the Vikings knew the type of birds, and approximately the distance they normally fly from the colony, they would have had a good estimate how far off land they were.

There were a number of additional signs the Vikings used to tell them that their ship was approaching land. Spotting stationary clouds—usually over islands or high mountains—when surrounding clouds are moving can be an important clue. The stationary clouds may indicate land which was not yet visible. The color of the sea could have also been used for information. A brown or grayish color indicates a river run out. Sometimes the current can carry the color far out to sea. The sound of the surf, and other sounds can also be heard at great distances. Sounds and odors would have been helpful, particularly in periods of reduced visibility. Odors, such as from wild fire caused by a lightning strike, can be detected far out to sea.

The current south of Iceland branches to form the Irminger and Norway currents. The Irminger current curves toward the north and northwest to join the East Greenland Current southwest of Iceland.

The Norway current continues in a northeasterly direction along the coast of Norway. The ship would have stayed on a westerly course until the navigator sighted the high mountains on the southeast coast of Greenland.

The seabirds still gather in great number along the coast.

When the navigator sighted this landmark, he was about 95 nautical miles off the coast. The course was changed to southwest to follow the coastline and at the same time take advantage of the East Greenland current that flows in a southwesterly direction.

After the course change, coastal navigation was used for the rest of the voyage using known landmarks in the area to guide them towards their destination. Off Kap Farvel, at the southern tip of Greenland, the East Greenland current curves sharply to the northwest, following the coastline. It becomes known as the West Greenland current. The navigator continued to take advantage of this current when the ship was heading for either the Eastern Settlement (Austurbyggð) or the Western Settlement (Vesturbyggð), by following the coastline and current. Today both the east and west Greenland currents are some times known by the single name: Greenland Current.

The distance from the Beinisvörd Cliffs, Faeroe Island, to Kap Farvel, Greenland, is about 1,126 nautical miles. When the ship was abeam Kap

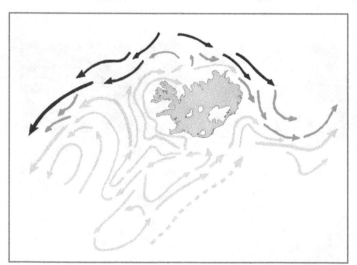

Farvel and the area was ice free, the navigator changed course to northwest and headed straight for Herjolfsness, about six hours sailing from Kap Farvel. From abeam Kap Farvel to Herjolfsness it is about 36 nautical miles. This was an ideal voyage when everything went well. But

The ocean currents around Iceland. Darker represents colder.
Data from Hafrannsöknastofnunin Marine Research Institute
Reykjavik, Iceland

if they ran into trouble, rough weather, storms, overcast, and fog, then they had to depend on their dead reckoning. Dead reckoning means to determine the ship's whereabouts by using the courses steered, distance run, and the influences of current and wind. This was the real test of the navigator's skill. Without the sun or stars to guide them the Viking navigators had to depend on their memory for courses steered by the wind or swell, and the approximate distance run in terms of days until the sun came out again, or until the stars were visible at night.

Conclusion

The Vikings where excellent seamen, navigators, traders, boatbuilders, woodcarvers, and explorers. They also had great knowledge of coastal navigation, using known landmarks from place to place. They sailed in the Baltic area, the great rivers of Eastern Europe, the Black Sea, and into the Mediterranean. Later they explored the Shetlands, Orkneys, Hebrides, Isle of Man, the main British Isles, then onto the Færøs, Iceland, and Greenland.

When crossing the North Atlantic, they used land and seamarks such as islands, snow covered mountains, birds and whales for references. They used the sun and stars for references when visible, and steered by the wind and swell when the sun and stars were not visible.

Whales were one animal that could be an indicator of location for the Viking navigator.

Several North Atlantic sailing directions from the Viking age are preserved in the Icelandic sagas. The stars, such as zenith stars, were used in the spring and fall during the sailing season. We know that Polaris was mentioned in the sagas. We also know that their ship design improved throughout the Viking age, as did their skill in navigation as they sailed farther and farther westward, finally on to the east coast of North America.

The sagas tell us that both King Olav the Stout (St. Olav), and Bishop Gudmund were in possession of the sunstone, and they both made ocean voyages. We are also told that Hrafn Sveinbjarnarson had the sunstone. Hrafn made ocean voyages between Iceland and Norway sometimes with Bishop Gudmund. Since Hrafn was a seafaring man and a navigator, he most likely carried the sunstone on these trips to be used for navigation.

There are still many outstanding questions to be answered about Viking navigation; clues will one day be found in a Viking burial mound, or perhaps in a sunken Viking ship that will give us more information. Hopefully the sunstone will be one of the objects found. One thing that is certain—the sunstone does work as a navigational aid when it is used properly, and there is every reason to believe the Vikings could have mastered its use.

The reconstructed Viking settlement in Newfoundland at L'Anse aux Meadows preserves the first historic traces of a European presence in the Americas—the ruins of a Norse settlement from the eleventh century, with wood and sod houses similar to those found in Norway.

A Norwegian team in 1960, led by Helge and Anne Stine Ingstad, discovered the site. Helge met a local fisherman, George Decker, who showed him what locals thought was an aboriginal camp. Excavation of the site later unearthed the Viking settlement. Some historians think the L'Anse aux Meadows area might be the site of the Norse Saga's Vinland. However, the description of the environment given in the sagas, plus navigational and botanical clues suggest a different location for Vinland.

New Land to the West—from the Grænlendinga Saga:

"There was now great talk of discovering new countries, Leif, the son of Eirik the Red of Brattahlid, went to see Bjarni Herjolfsson and bought his ship from him, and engaged a crew of 35. Leif asked his father Eirik to lead this expedition too, but Eirik was rather reluctant: he said he was getting old, and could endure hardships less easily than he used to. Leif replied that Eirik would still command more luck than any of his kinsmen. And in the end, Eirik let Leif have his way.

As soon as they were ready, Eirik rode off to the ship that was only a short distance away, but the horse he was riding stumbled and he was thrown, injuring his leg. "I am not meant to discover more countries than this one we now live in, said Eirik. This is as far as we go together."

Eirik returned to Brattahlid, but Leif went onboard the ship with his crew of 35. Among them was a southerner called Tyrkir. They made their ship ready and put out to sea. The first landfall they made was the country that Bjarni had sighted last. Then Leif said "Now we have done better than Bjarni where this country is concerned, we at least have set foot on it."

CHAPTER TWENTY

Where Was Vinland?

Vinland is the name Viking explorer Leif Eiriksson gave to the new land—now known as North America—that he and his men first set foot on around the year 1000. The name can refer to the entire region, and also to the first settlement established in the new land. In this discussion, I am seeking an answer to the puzzle of where the settlement was located.

Even before Leif Eiriksson's time, the Vikings had sailed from Norway through Gibraltar and all the way to the eastern Mediterranean. They had crossed the North Atlantic Ocean and settled in Iceland and Greenland. Archeological records now prove that they also continued the additional much shorter distance to reach the American continent.

The Viking settlers in Iceland, Greenland and Newfoundland knew about all of these voyages. There is no reason to believe that they stopped at Newfoundland, but rather that they pushed much farther south into the newly discovered land.

The distance from Newfoundland to New York is only one fifth of the distance they had sailed from Europe. Once the first Vikings reached Newfoundland, there was then pressure on the next Viking explorer to go farther. Leif was prodded by the stories told by Bjarni Herjolfsson. He likely wanted to be sure that he went farther south than Bjarni did. Throughout maritime history, sea captains and the sailors they commanded have been fiercely competitive, the Vikings were no exception.

By following the westward route from Greenland, Leif arrived at what is now known as North America—Leif called it Vinland. Leif Eiriksson sailed the course Bjarni Herjolfsson and his crew were on when Bjarni had accidently discovered North America while looking for Greenland, but Leif Eiriksson sailed in reverse, starting from Greenland and ending in North America. He would have encountered the same landmarks seen by Bjarni Herjolfsson, but in reverse order. This was probably how the sailing directions in the North Atlantic started. The story was passed on from person to person by word of mouth, until various routes in the North Atlantic became well known. By the end of the fourteenth century, the main sailing directions for the North Atlantic area were written down in the Icelandic sagas. These directions were based upon sea stories told by the experienced men sitting around the open fire during the long stormy winter nights.

Leif Eiriksson is said to have found three lands. He named them Helluland (Baffin Island), Markland (Labrador), and Vinland.

There is evidence from well known sources that L' Anse aux Meadows (Newfoundland) not only was used as a stepping stone to the entrance of the Gulf of Saint Lawrence, it was also used as a base on their way to and from Greenland and Vinland.

The sagas say that Leif and his men found more and larger salmon in Vinland than they had seen before. The Canadian archaeologist Catherine Carlson (1996) believes that in the eleventh century there were no salmon in Maine, or farther south, due to the warmer temperatures at that time. The rivers in the southern regions of the Gulf of Saint Lawrence, however, abounded with salmon. (Vikings of the North Atlantic Saga, Smithsonian.) In contrast, National Oceanic & Atmospheric Administration gives the traditional range of Atlantic salmon as: *"The historic North American range of Atlantic salmon extended from the rivers of Ungava Bay, Canada, to Long Island Sound."* (John Kocik and Russell Brown, NOAA paper.) Different experts, different conclusions.

The sagas also mention that they found grapes in Vinland. Assuming that the grapes from the sagas are meant to be American wild grapes (Vitis riparia), the saga lands could have been located over a large expanse, as the grape's distribution is wide. It is found in New Brunswick and northern Quebec to Manitoba and Montana, south to Tennessee, northern Texas, Colorado, and

Utah, from the Atlantic to the Rockies and all areas in between; not much help here in pinning down the location.

The sagas also refer to "self-sown wheat," which probably refers to wild rye (Elymus virginicus). Wild rye occurs in roughly the same area and also coincides with the northern limit of butternut, (Juglans cinerea), a form of walnut that was found at the L'Anse aux Meadows site and most likely brought there by the Norse, according to Gísli Sigurðsson, of the Smithsonian.

Here is what the sagas say about the tides at Leif's arrival in Vinland. *"They steered a westerly course round the headland. There were extensive shallows there and at low tide their ship was left high and dry, the sea almost out of sight. But they were so impatient to land that they could not bear to wait for the rising tide to float the ship; they ran ashore to a place where the river flowed out of a lake. A soon as the tide had re-floated the ship they brought her into the lake, where they anchored her."* What is being described here is a tidal flat—a body of salt water along the shoreline that is so shallow that the bottom is exposed at low tides. A ship could not be floated except at high tide. This tidal flat evidentially covered a large area as the sea was "almost out of sight" as the tide went out.

To summarize: important clues that point to the location of Leif Eiriksson's Vinland are these:

¤ The whole winter went by without temperatures below the freezing point, and without snow. This indicates that they were farther south than Canada, or that the climate was warmer along the entire North America coast at that time.

¤ They found wild grain growing. The impression is one of grassy meadows and forests.

¤ They observed "more and larger salmon than they had seen before." The exact historic range of Atlantic salmon is debated, but the general distribution was probably a region from the Saint Lawrence Basin, to at least southern New England.

¤ The grass mostly stayed green year-round, even in the middle of winter, also indicating a milder climate.

¤ Wild grapes were found in abundance. Wild grapes range over much of North America.

¤ Navigating into the lake where the settlement was located required passage up a river that flowed with the tides. At low tide there was a extensive tidal flat off the coast that could cause the ships to run aground.

¤ The winter days and nights were of more equal length than the Vikings were used to experiencing, indicating a more southern latitude.

¤ On the shortest day of the year (winter solstice) the sun passed through *eykt*arstad before dropping below the horizon at sunset. (*More on this on the next page.*)

¤ At Newfoundland's L'Anse aux Meadows there was found butternuts that are not native to Newfoundland, but are native to New England.

One place along the Atlantic coast of North America that fits these clues is Cape Cod, Massachusetts. In a mild winter, the climate is as described, the tides and navigational features are correct, the latitude is at 41° N, which is within the location for the sunset described in the saga, and of course the island across from the south shore of Cape Cod still carries in its name a botanical clue: Martha's Vineyard, where wild grapes still grow to this day.

But there is evidence to suggest other locations as well. Several places along the shores of the Gulf of Saint Lawrence fit the saga description of the place where Leif and his men landed: a saltwater tidal flat, with a river leading to an inland lake. There were abundant salmon in this area, and the grapes could have been found here—especially if the climate was warmer then. (*See Appendix 8 for a discussion on climate change.*)

There is also no way to be totally sure about the time of day when the Vikings were observing the sunset mentioned in the saga reference. The sun was still shining when it passed through *eyktarstad*, and it set sometime later.

Below is a diagram that compares sunset at Cape Cod with the sunset at the Bay of Saint Lawrence for the winter solstice around the year 1000. The observer is looking south with the sun setting generally in the southwest as described in the statement from the saga: *"In this country, night and day were of more even length than in either Greenland or Iceland. The sun passed the points of eyktarstad and dagmalsstad in the period of the shortest day."* (Winter solstice.)

In modern times, the time of sunset for any date, at any location on earth may simply be looked up in nautical tables. In the time of the Vikings, such tables were not available. On the next page we will explain the time and location of the sunset reference as the Vikings understood it.

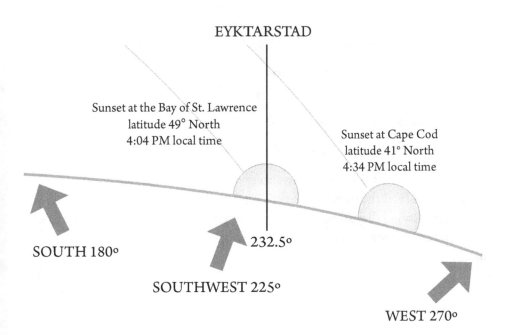

EYKTARSTAD

Sunset at the Bay of St. Lawrence
latitude 49° North
4:04 PM local time

Sunset at Cape Cod
latitude 41° North
4:34 PM local time

232.5°

SOUTH 180°

SOUTHWEST 225°

WEST 270°

Using the Viking *Eykt* to Find the Settlement's Location

The Grænlendinga saga describes Leif Eiriksson's statement that sunset at Vinland came *after* the sun had passed *Eykt* (*eyktarstad*) and sunrise came before *dagmalsstad* on the shortest day of the year, the winter solstice. The statement goes as follows:

> *"Meira var þar jafndægri en a Grænlandia eða Íslandi.*
> *Sól hafði þar eyktarstað og dagmálsstad um skammdegi."*

The translation reads: "In this country, night and day were of more even length than in either Greenland or Iceland. The sun passed the points of *eyktarstad* and *dagmalsstad* in the period of the shortest day."

Assume for the moment that the sunset took place right at *eykt*. We can determine bearing in degrees, to the solstice sunset (and sunrise) by calculating the angles from the *áttirs*. Refer to the diagram on the next page.

First take the distance westward from south to the end of *Suder*. This is 22.5°. Then the sun has to pass through two parts in the *Utsuder* section 15° x 2 = 30°. This will bring us to *Eykt* (22.5° + 30°)= 52.5° west of south.

This gives us the true bearing to the sunrise (at *dagmalsstad*) and sunset (at *eyktarstad*) on the shortest day of the year.

True bearing at sunset: 180°+52.5°=232.5°

True bearing at sunrise: 180°-52.5°=127.5°

Now we can use this bearing to interpolate the latitude at which the Vikings observed the sunset. The difference in the bearing found above and due west is called the "amplitude" of the sun. Using the amplitude, we can look up the latitude in tables that relate the latitude to the amplitude. (*See table page 154.*)

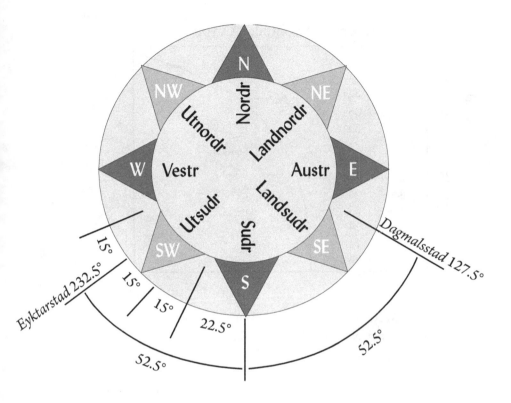

The table is based on the mathematical relationship of this formula:

$$\sin \text{(amplitude)} = \frac{\sin \text{(declination)}}{\cos \text{(latitude)}}$$

For our situation, the true bearing to the *eyktarstad* sunset was found to be 232.5°

The associated amplitude of the sun for the bearing of 232.5° is 270° (West) minus 232.5° or 37.5°. On the table, a vertical line from 37.5° will cross the curve showing latitude at about 49° North. This is the latitude of the Bay of Saint Lawrence, and marks the northern limit of the range of possibilities for Vinland.

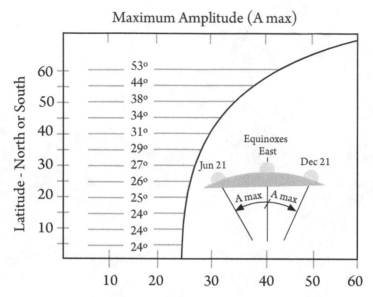

Maximum Amplitude (A max)

Sun's Maximum Amplitude based on chart from
Emergency Navigation *by David Burch.*

It is of interest to note that at 41° N, the latitude of Cape Cod, the amplitude of the sun on the winter solstice is 31.8°, corresponding to a sunset of 30 minutes after the sun passed *Eykt*.

The location of the first Vinland settlement can be stated as somewhere on the Atlantic coast of North America, between the Saint Lawrence Basin to the north, and Long Island Sound to the south. Within this range, there are scholars who champion one location over another; with every passing season, some new piece of evidence is brought forth to fortify some site as being the "correct" one. Until some real object is found that positively identifies the site, we can only be sure that the Vikings were here—in number and for longer than most people realize—and without doubt their Vinland settlement was the first European colony in America.

The "Vinland Map" at Yale University

The "Vinland Map," possibly the first map showing the New World, is currently housed in Yale University's Beinecke Rare Book and Manuscript Library. The map shows Europe (including Scandinavia), Northern Africa, Asia and the Far East, all of which were known by 15th-century travelers. In the northwest Atlantic Ocean, however, it also shows the "Island of Vinland." Text on the map reads, in part: *"By God's will, after a long voyage from the island of Greenland to the south toward the most distant remaining parts of the western ocean sea, sailing southward amidst the ice, the companions Bjarni and Leif Eiriksson discovered a new land, extremely fertile and even having vines, ... which island they named Vinland."*

In a scientific paper published in the August 2002 issue of the journal Radiocarbon, Scientists from the University of Arizona, the U.S. Department of Energy's Brookhaven National Laboratory, and the Smithsonian Institution, disclose how they used carbon-dating technology to determine the age of the parchment that comprises the so-called "Vinland Map" at Yale University. The scientists concluded that the Vinland Map parchment dates to approximately 1434, or nearly 60 years before Christopher Columbus set foot in the West Indies.

Many scholars have agreed that if the Vinland Map is authentic, it is the first known cartographic representation of North America, and its date would be key in establishing the history of European knowledge of the lands bordering the western Atlantic Ocean. Garman Harbottle, the lead Brookhaven researcher on the project stated. "If it is, in fact, a forgery, then the forger was surely one of the most skillful criminals ever to pursue that line of work."

The map, drawn in ink and measuring 10 x 16 inches (27.8 x 41.0 cm), surfaced in Europe in the mid 1950s, but had no distinct record of prior ownership or provenance in any famous library. The map and the accompanying "Tartar Relation," a manuscript of undoubted authenticity that was at some point bound with the Vinland Map in book form, were purchased in 1958 for $1 million by Paul A. Mellon, known for his many important gifts to Yale, and, at Mellon's request, subjected to an exhaustive six-year investigation.

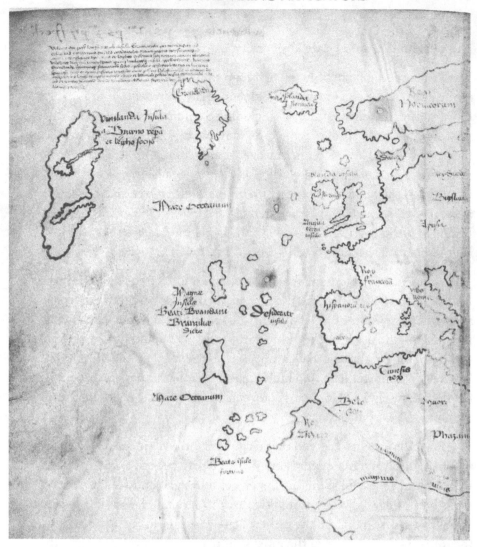

A portion of the Vinland Map from Yale University's Beinecke Rare Book and Manuscript Library. The map shows Vinland as an island, probably because at the early date of its origin the Vikings had not explored beyond the coastline of the new land. Used with permission.

In 1965 the Yale University Press published "The Vinland Map and the Tartar Relation," a detailed study by R.A. Skelton, T. E. Marston and G. D. Painter that firmly argued for the map's authenticity, connecting it with the Catholic Church's Council of Basel (1431-1449), which was convened a half-century before Columbus' voyage. Two scientific conferences, in 1966 and 1996, featured strong debates over the map's authenticity, but no final determination could be made based on the available facts. The new analysis of the map parchment reaffirms the association with the Council of Basel because it dates exactly to that time period and makes a strong case for the map's authenticity.

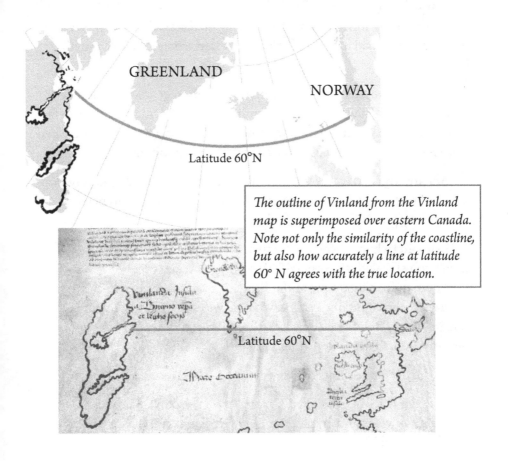

GREENLAND

NORWAY

Latitude 60°N

The outline of Vinland from the Vinland map is superimposed over eastern Canada. Note not only the similarity of the coastline, but also how accurately a line at latitude 60° N agrees with the true location.

Latitude 60°N

Tyrkir finds grapes—

Leif names the new land

One evening in the settlement Leif had established, it was found that one of the older crewmen was missing. Tyrkir, called "the southerner," could not be found. Leif was very worried by this. Tyrkir had stayed with Leif's father for a long time, and had even looked after Leif when Leif was a small boy.

Leif spoke angrily to the other men, and left to go and look for Tyrkir, taking twelve men with him as a search party. They had not gone too far from the house when Tyrkir came towards them shouting greetings. Leif was relieved to see that his foster-father was in a good mood.

Apparently, Tyrkir was not an attractive fellow. He had a sharply sloping forehead, and a dark and swarthy look—seedy in appearance—but he was very good at all kinds of odd jobs.

Leif said to him, "Why were you so long gone foster-father, and why didn't you stay with the others?" Tyrkir began to answer, but was speaking German for a long time and rolling his eyes, laughing and grinning, so that no one could understand what he was saying. After a while he said in Norse, "I didn't go much farther than you did, but I have some news for you. I have found vines and grapes."

"Is it true, foster-father?" asked Leif.

"Of course it's true," replied Tyrkir, "I was born in a place where there are plenty of vines and grapes." So Leif decided to call the new land they had discovered Vinland.

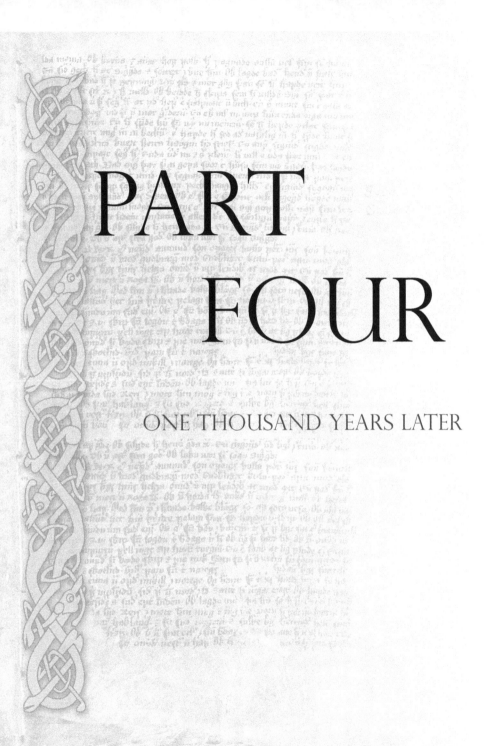

PART FOUR

ONE THOUSAND YEARS LATER

"The Gods do not deduct from man's allotted span those hours spent in sailing."
-Ancient Phoenician Proverb

CHAPTER TWENTY ONE

1000 YEARS LATER...

Voyages on the "Borgundknarren" Viking Ship Replica

Voyage One

A few years ago, I had the wonderful opportunity to sail on a replica of an ancient Viking ship using a *rå* (square) sail as the Vikings did. This was on a reproduction of an ocean going *knarr* ship, the "Borgundknarren" from Sunnmøre Museum in Ålesund, Norway. The "Borgundknarren" is an exact replica of a Viking ship found about 20 km north of Roskilde, Denmark.

I sailed on the *knarr* as a crew-member in the fall of 1996, on a two-day trip from Ålesund to Aukra and back, and then again in the summer of 1997, on a seven-day round trip between Ålesund and Trondheim, to celebrate Trondheim's 1000-year anniversary.

I signed on one weekend in September for my first voyage. Per Weddegjerde was the captain, Sigbjørn, Ove, Runar, Lars, Svein Ove, Margit and Arve, Atle, and a few others were crew members.

A clinker built hull where each plank overlaps the next.

The carved wooden nameplate honors the
"Borgundkarren" knarr replica.

Once I was there and really on board the "Borgundknarren," I could
not believe that I was a crew member on a real Viking ship sailing with real
Viking seamen from the west coast of Norway, where most of the settlers to
Iceland came from. One of the crew members told me later that I was smiling from ear to ear when I came on board. To sail on a Viking ship replica
was for me a dream come true—no wonder that I was showing a happy face
when I came on board.

There was also another boat, but smaller, an *åttering*, which is a type of
boat that is rigged for sail and has eight oars. The plan was to sail from Ålesund to Aukra to pick up an old fishing vessel, the "Havdrønn", that was built
in Bjørkedalen. The fishing vessel was later to be shipped to Bjørkedalen for
restoration.

Finally, both the *knarr* and the *åttering* were ready and we left the dock
at the museum in Ålesund. One modern necessary addition was a small
engine in the stern for manuvering in harbors and for emergencies. Both the
knarr and the *åttering* were sailing under power because there is no place to
maneuver in the narrows on the way out.

When we came out to Valderhaugsfjorden we stopped the engine and set
the sail. Our course was for Valderøya. It looked like it was going to be a nice
passage.

This was strictly a coastwise voyage. We navigated by using a compass to
steer by, and a bearing compass to take bearings of markers, landmarks, and
light houses. The captain assigned jobs for everybody, but he had a good experienced crew from before, so everything went smoothly. My job on board

was to help set the sail; adjusting it as needed when going from one tack to another. I also was assigned to steer from time to time. Steering was something I liked the most. I could feel the power from the square sail. It does not take much wind to make the *knarr* move.

The weather was overcast and rainy. I talked about the sunstone and explained how it works, and was hoping for the rain to quit so I could demonstrate the stone for everybody on board. We needed just a small patch of blue sky in the morning or evening in order to take the bearing, but there was no break in the clouds.

Our companion ship, the *åttering* had engine trouble. After several tries to get the engines working, they gave up. The *åttering* was taken in tow and we all came in to a place called Longva where we spent the night at Lars and Per's place, an old store that they had changed into a guesthouse. There were 18 overnight guests from the two boats. Outside the wind had picked up with heavy rain, so it was good to be in port that night where it was nice and warm.

The next morning after breakfast everybody went on board the *knarr* since the *åttering* refused to start. We towed the ship to the harbor of Rogne near Longva and left it there.

We arrived at our next stop, Røssøyvågen, without any problems. We expected to take delivery of the Havdrønn shortly after arrival and then head back to Ålesund. We tried to start the motor onboard the Havdrønn, but after three years of sitting in one place, she was not cooperative at all. Our crew included an expert from the museum who had experience with this type of engine, Svein Ove Flaten. After nearly three hours of trying and trying to start the engine, the captain on the *knarr* said, "Let's go." Jakob Bjørkedalen asked, "Are you in such a hurry?" Then they decided to give it one more try. All of a sudden the engine started with a big bang. Black smoke came pouring out of the engine room, and so did Svein Ove, covered with soot. Other than that, he was fine. It was a triumph to get the engine started after three years of it being idle.

With the engine running on the Havdrønn, Per decided it was time to head on back to Ålesund. The sail went up in a hurry and everybody was looking forward to a nice run under sail towards the Lepsøyrevet and back to

163

the museum. Havdrønn was dropping back, but still running. After a while she slowed down more and more until she finally came to a full stop.

The engine was overheating. Per said, "Down with the sail" and the sail was dropped. The motor was started on the *knarr*. We turned around and took Havdrønn in tow for the duration of the voyage back to Ålesund.

We were now heading south in the Harøyfjorden, the weather was nice, and I could set up to take a bearing of the sun with the sunstone. By this time we had sailed alongside a large island and the sun had just set behind the ridge. The zenith over head was clear. One of the sailors asked, "How can you take a bearing when you can't even see the sun?" I told him this was a good time and a perfect situation, with a clear zenith and no glare on the stone from the sun. A bearing was taken with the sunstone and it pointed to the hidden sun. A compass sighting of the sunstone's bearing was also taken to confirm that the sunstone was showing a true bearing.

The sunstone was tested on several occasions during the voyage. Each crew member took turns to confirm the true bearing of the sun. Compass sighting of the sunstone's bearing was also taken to confirm that the sunstone was always showing a true bearing.

We arrived at the Sunnmøre Museum around midnight with the Havdrønn safely secured to our port side. A Viking replica ship works pretty good as a tow vessel.

I donated a sunstone to the crew members from Sykkylven. They told me the stone will stay with the president of their club. I told Per, the captain, that he would have a sunstone for the museum the next year, when I return to Norway.

On our way back towards Ålesund and the museum, the weather became nicer and nicer. Around Lepsøyrevet the wind died and the sea was still. It was a beautiful evening with a full moon. Away from any cities or any man-made lights the sky was astonishing. The Big Dipper was especially bright and clear, showing off all of it's stars. I kept thinking about what a beacon the Viking navigators had directly overhead.

A thousand years ago there were the four zenith stars they used, but today there is only one, namely Dubhe, with a declination of N61° 44′. Dubhe is the zenith star for Ålesund, 62° 28′N, Ytterøyane 61° 34′N, Florø 61° 36′N, Kvanhovden 61° 42′N, and Stattlandet 62° 11′N, all in Norway, and for Thorshavn 62° 00′N, and Suderoy 61° 36′N, in the Faeroe islands.

An observer's zenith star passes directly over him once every twenty four hours. The zenith passage of a star follows its line of declination, equivalent to latitude on earth. The star is as many degrees north or south of the celestial equator as the observer is from the earth's equator. For example: on a voyage between Thorshavn, Faeroe, and Stattlandet, Norway, Dubhe—with a declination of N61° 44′—can be used as a Zenith star.

With the sky as clear as it was for our passage, the Vikings could have easily found their way home.

Voyage Two

In the end of June, 1997, I received a call from Per Weddegjerde, the captain of the Borgundknarren. Once again I was invited to make a voyage on board the Borgundknarren, sailing from the museum in Ålesund to Trondheim, Norway to celebrate Trondheim's 1000-year anniversary. Who in their right mind can say no to an opportunity like that? And of course, the answer was a big "Yes! I will be there the day before departure." I had to get my airline ticket from Seattle to Ålesund right away because there was not much time left. The date for sailing was set for the 17th of July.

A few days later Per called again and told me the sailing date was changed to monday, the 14th of July. I told Per I would make it no matter what it takes to get there. I had to change my tickets and hope there would be room on the flight at an earlier date with only three days notice; luckily there was room.

I arrived in Ålesund Sunday the 13th, 1997, in the late afternoon. I joined the ship early on Monday morning. It was good to be back aboard the *knarr* and meet up with previous and new crew members. Again Per was the captain for the voyage. We also had families of some of the crew aboard on this trip. This time our voyage was to be a round-trip of seven days.

In the early morning hours, all kinds of activities took place on the dock at the museum and onboard the *knarr* and *åttering* —the same one that had engine trouble and was left behind for repairs the last time I sailed on the "Borgundknarren." The two vessels were getting ready to set sail for Nidaros (the old name for Trondheim). All kinds of things were piling up on the dock ready to be taken aboard the ships. There were ship chests with period clothing to be used on arrival in Trondheim, photo equipment, modern navigation equipment, fuel, provisions and other supplies. Finally everything was stowed aboard. The weather was tropical—sweltering—nearly unheard of weather for Norway.

While we were sailing, Margit and some of the women decided to cook a special meal from the West Coast area of Norway. It was a type of potato dumpling called *potetball*, that was boiled in a pot on a little sterno camp stove. It was delicious.

We arrived at Børøysund for the night. Since the *knarr* is an open Viking ship, we had to rig canvas over the deck to create what we thought would be a dry sleeping area. However, during the night the fog seeped in and made everything, including the crew, pretty wet anyway. Luckily, we had tropical weather, so the night was fairly warm, and there were no complaints from anyone.

During the night the Viking ship Olav Tryggvason came gliding in towards the dock, silently coming out of the fog like a ghost ship, and docked behind the åttring. The Olav Tryggvason is similar to the Gokstad ship, but smaller in size. This beautiful little ship had a nicely carved dragon head on the prow. They were also heading for the festivities in Trondheim.

On Wednesday, July 16th we left Børøysund at 1100 (11AM), again under power, heading for a place called Austrått. It was another hot day. Light wind was predicted. Towards Ørlandet the wind picked up and the sail went up, but it didn't last, and we dropped the sail and started the engines once again. We arrived in Austrått around 1600 (4PM). The temperature was at least 30°C (86°F). There were all kinds of historic ships and boats at the dock, all destined for Trondheim. This was the last stop. We visited with some of the other crews and admired their ships.

Thursday, July 17th was again another beautiful, hot and sweltering day. We started the last leg of the trip to Trondheim at 1000 (10AM). Some of the other ships had already left earlier, and some were still making preparations to get underway. This time we had wind at about 15-18 knots, so we were at last able to set sail properly. Then the wind decreased for a while until we passed Agdenes light, close to Trondheim. From then on it was good sailing into Trondheim. We sailed into the Kanalhavna (the channel) in Trondheim and docked at Fosenkaia, close to the railroad station. It was quite a sight to see the gathering of the historic ships and boats, reminiscent of the Viking years in Trondheim when they gathered together at that center of trade. There were people lined up on both sides of the canal to welcome the arrival of all the ships and boats coming for the 1000-year celebration. The dock was full of merchants and booths selling and trading pottery, carvings, handmade knives, handcrafted jewelry, leather goods, 12-foot and longer rowboats, food, and everything else imaginable.

Friday, July 18th was the big day everybody had been waiting for; a sailing regatta. We all sailed around Munkholmen, an island off Trondheim, just a short distance and visible from the city. We all had to demonstrate the "man-overboard" drill. One of our women on board took the drill seriously. She had changed into her bathing suit, and next thing we knew, she was ready to jump overboard to be "rescued." Per, the captain, stopped her at the last minute from jumping into the sea. Per explained, "We don't really ask someone to jump overboard when we practice the drill." She walked away very disappointed. She was a strong swimmer and loved to swim, but the captain prevailed.

Saturday, July 19th had more races and demonstrations scheduled for the smaller boats. We didn't take part in these activities. It was free time for our crew. I set up a series of demonstrations of the use of the sunstone for the public. In the evening there was a dinner party in a big tent with lots of food, drink, and speeches, followed with music and dancing.

July 20th was our departure day from Trondheim. The festivities in Trondheim continued; we had to make way in the harbor for the tall ships that had begun to arrive. Before we left, a few of our crew members left the ship, and the rest of us set sail back for our home port. The trip going back to Ålesund was nearly identical to voyage to Trondheim, except this time we hit dense fog during the day. The last night we stayed at Håholmen, Ragnar Thorseth's guesthouse. He was the captain on the "Saga Siglar," another replica of a *knarr* identical to the "Borgundknarren." He had sailed "Saga Siglar" around the world in two-and-one-half years.

The next day we continued our voyage to Ålesund with our arrival in the evening. Per let me get off the ship at a dock about 100 feet from my hotel in Ålesund, the *knarr* continued back to its home at the museum.

My wife and daughter arrived in Ålesund a few hours later by the coastwise passenger ship. I met them at the dock. My wife commented on my appearance. She saw all the bruises I sustained by banging into the rigging. She noted the 15 pounds I lost when she saw may pants hanging from my belt in folds. According to her, I looked tired, but boy did I have fun. It was a wonderful experience.

Sunstone Facts

During World War II Iceland spar was a strategic mineral used for the sighting equipment of bombardiers on bombers. *(See appendix 2.)*

Inlaid calcite was used on the throne found in the Tomb of Tutankhamun in Egypt, dated from 1340 B.C.

Double refraction in calcite was discovered in 1669 by Erasmus Bartholinus (Denmark).

In 1828 William Nicol (Scotland), invented a polarizing prism made from two calcite components. The device became known subsequently as a "Nicol prism."

Iceland spar is available in rock shops around the world, in large quantities and at affordable prices. However, most of today's so called Iceland spar comes from Mexico. It is the clear calcite from Iceland that best demonstrates the unique property of double refraction.

CHAPTER TWENTY TWO
1000 YEARS LATER...

The Quest for an Icelandic Sunstone

After a successful voyage on the Viking ship replica, there was still one more thing to do. In order to complete my research about the sunstone, I needed to make a trip to Iceland to see for myself if the stone was available to the Vikings. For years I had planned to visit the southeast coast of Iceland. In the summer of 1999 my wife and I set out to do just that.

From the sagas we know that the Vikings sailed from Stad, Norway to Horn, Iceland. We decided to go to Höfn to look for Iceland spar, since it is located in the same general area as Horn. Because there is no archaeological proof or evidence that the Vi-

Weathered Iceland spar with gravel in the scree.

kings were mining Iceland spar, the main objective of the trip to Iceland was to confirm that the Vikings could have obtained the sunstone in the scree or on the ground and then used it for navigation.

In Höfn we stayed in a guesthouse operated by a young couple. We talked to the innkeeper about Iceland spar. He suggested that we check out the local museum. He knew they had a few pieces on display, from both the Helgustaðir and Hoffell areas.

The next day the innkeeper told us that he had contacted a man with the name of Gisli and that he was going to stop by the guesthouse to talk to us. Gisli turned out to be the best contact for sunstones we could have ever found. He told us that he had worked in a Iceland spar mine in 1937, and he knew about all there is to know about Iceland spar. He invited us to his home to look at his local rock collection. He showed us his stones which included fine specimens of Iceland spar from the old mine. I asked Gisli if it was possible to find Iceland spar on the ground or in the scree. The answer was "yes."

On the trail up the mountain to the source of the Iceland spar in Iceland.

The innkeeper and Gisli said we should drive into the mountains near Hoffell where Gisli would show us the place he had worked in 1937. The Innkeeper said we would need a four-wheel drive car to go there. When an Icelander tells you "you need a four- wheel drive" he really means it. I asked him where can we get a car on such a short notice. He told me it would be difficult this time of the year, because the place is full of tourists and most cars are rented. To our surprise he said, "I will take you there because now I am interested too."

In the afternoon Gisli, the innkeeper, my wife, and I left for the mountain. After some rough driving on gravel roads with several unbridged rivers and streams and then cross-country where there were no roads, we arrived safely at our destination.

With his cane and backpack in place, Gisli took the lead ready to climb. We started up the mountain side towards the camp site where Gisli worked in his younger days. We climbed up to a plateau about 400 feet up the mountain, to Gisli's old working place. He showed us a pile of small scraps of Iceland spar that were broken off from the larger pieces. They had used this place to clean up the pieces of Iceland spar before sending them down to the bottom of the mountain for packing and shipment—Gisli explained the whole operation to us.

On our way down from the mountain, Gisli pointed out numerous pieces of Iceland spar that had washed out of the vein higher in the mountain and then tumbled down the mountain in the scree. Some of the stones were clear and shiny where they had broken along the facets of the crystal as they fell. Others had an opaque surface due to weathering and abrasion.

Many of the pieces we saw were at least 1.5 x 2 x 1 inches (4 x 5 x 3 cm)—large and clear enough to be used for navigation.

Now I know that sunstones suitable for use in navigation could and still can be found lying on the ground in Iceland. The Vikings could have easily found these stones during their explorations.

Until fairly recently, clear Iceland spar was used in the manufacturer of polarizing prisms and other optical equipment. Occasionally rough crystals were used in jewelry or as ornaments.

Iceland spar is now protected in Iceland. It is strictly forbidden to remove anything from the old mines. The mine at Helgustaðir was put under protection order as a natural monument in 1975.

A POSTSCRIPT

Icelandic Spar Crystal is Discovered in Ancient Shipwreck

Just as this book was going to press, I was made aware of a remarkable discovery. I received an astonishing communication from the European based Wreckshed Research Team. This team is composed of eminent archaeologists, historians, scientists and other professionals who are exploring an old shipwreck in the English Channel. This ship dates back to the Elizabethan period (1548 to 1604). The group has recovered a piece of semi-opaque crystal, found among 2500 other artifacts and fragment on the bottom.

The researchers contacted me to share their findings because they were wondering if this crystal is the same type of crystal that I have been researching in relationship to Viking navigation. From the description of the stone and the pictures that they sent to me, I have concluded that it is the same mineral: Icelandic spar. This could turn out to be a find of considerable significance. While the ship at this site was not a Viking vessel, this is still an important find. This is the first recorded find of an Icelandic spar crystal in an ancient shipwreck.

Steve Wright, the diver who made the find, reports that the stone was near a pewter plate. He stated that there were many small fragments around the crystal, which may have been wood, which could possibly indicate a storage box.

The crystal that they recovered measures about 2 x 2 x 5 cm. The surface is opaque, probably due to almost 500 years of immersion in salt water. The sharp straight edges characteristic of the crystal have eroded somewhat, but the distinctive rhombohedral shape and angles are still obvious.

This find is not from the Viking Age, so we can't be sure it was used as a navigational tool. Its presence in the shipwreck could demonstrate the survival of ancient methods into the age of scientific navigation, or, as one of the Wreckshed Research Team pointed out, it might have been on board as a good luck charm from times past.

The magnetic compass was already in use in the Elizabethan era, but was not always reliable. The compass needle can vary from a few degrees to over 40 degrees away from true north, depending on one's location and local conditions. Compass variation is the difference in bearing between true north and magnetic north. Magnetic compasses are also subject to magnetic error. These old ships had a lot of iron onboard, such as cannons, which would mysteriously deflect the compass needle. The navigators could never be sure that the compass was pointing north. I can imagine how relieved an ancient navigator would be to have another reliable tool to check how much the compass was in error; he could then correct his course accordingly. A sunstone would be an excellent tool for checking for compass error on an Elizabethan ship, not provable for this particular ship but certainly plausible.

I have been hoping and waiting for someone to discover a navigational sunstone in an archaeological site. Is this a navigational sunstone? Will other sunstones be found at older sites that can be traced back to the Viking Age? More research is needed before the crystal that was found in this vessel can be unequivocally declared a navigational tool. Still, this is a very important and exciting discovery.

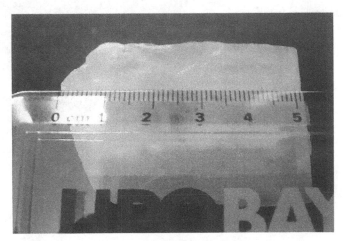

Measuring the crystal recovered by Wreckshed Research Team

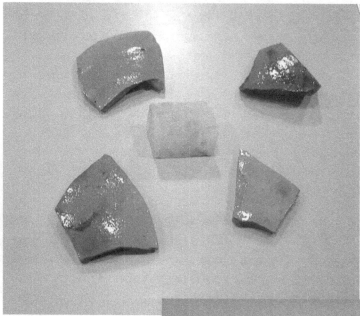

Above: the recovered calcite crystal with several pieces of a pottery jar found nearby.

Right: the diver who found the crystal—Steve Wright

Postscript Photos by: Jeffery K. Roff, H.R.D. Dia Used with kind permission of Alderney Wreckshed

I AM the God Thor,
I am the War God,
I am the Thunderer!
Here in my Northland,
My fastness and fortress, Reign I forever!

Here amid icebergs
Rule I the nations;
This is my hammer,
Miölner the mighty;
Giants and sorcerers Cannot withstand it!

These are the gauntlets
Wherewith I wield it,
And hurl it afar off;
his is my girdle;
Whenever I brace it, Strength is redoubled!

The light thou beholdest
Stream through the heavens,
In flashes of crimson,
Is but my red beard
Blown by the night-wind, Affrighting the nations!

Jove is my brother;
Mine eyes are the lightning;
The wheels of my chariot
Roll in the thunder,
The blows of my hammer Ring in the earthquake!

Force rules the world still,
Has ruled it, Shall rule it;
Meekness is weakness,
Strength is triumphant,
Over the whole earth Still is it Thor's-Day!

—Henry Wadsworth Longfellow

Appendix 1

Testing the Sunstone:

On August 12, 2002 at 20:31:37 local time, Seattle, Washington, USA, the sun had set behind a large building. The location of the sun was not visible. The zenith was clear. I had made a pedestal with a cutout hole for the sunstone, which sat on a mirror placed on a rotating wooden disk. Instead of holding the stone up in the air and bending my neck backwards to look through from underneath, I could just glance into the mirror to adjust the stone.

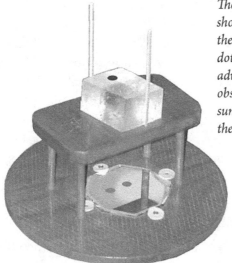

The author's sunstone stand showing the black dot on top of the stone and the reflected double dots in the mirror underneath. The advantage of this stand is that the observer does not need to hold the sunstone overhead and look up at the sky.

First, I lined up the stone toward the relative brightness of the evening sky. Then it was rotated until the double image was equal in value. After the bearing was taken, I used the Nautical-Almanac for the year 2002, and the sight reduction tables Pub. No. 249, Volume 3 to calculate the true bearing of the sun. The sunstone pointed to the hidden sun at 294° true, which agreed with the azimuth tables. For accurate results the stone must be kept level. If you check your sunstone bearing with a magnetic compass to verify the accuracy of the bearing, be sure there are no compass errors. Using a compass or sextant, one cannot expect much more accuracy than was obtained by using the sunstone.

Appendix 2

The Kollsman Sky Compass:

Sky compass defined: An instrument for determining azimuth of the sun by utilizing the polarization of sunlight in the sky.

"A sky compass indicates direction by means of the polarizing effect of the earth's atmosphere on sunlight. Unpolarized sunlight, upon entering the earth's atmosphere, is scattered and becomes plane polarized, its vibrations being in a plane perpendicular to the line from the sun to the observer. When the sun is on the horizon, this plane is vertical. By means of a suitable analyzer of Polaroid material and Cellophane, the sky compass detects this plane and the vertical plane which is perpendicular to it, or in the direction of the sun. A possible 90 degrees or 180 degrees ambiguity exists, but this is not of practical significance because the relative brightness of the sky indicates which of the four possible directions is toward the sun. The analyzer is then rotated until dark and light portions are of equal brightness. The sky compass is maintained with its face in a level position, pointing at the zenith, which must be clear and unobstructed for an accurate reading. The sun itself need not be visible, and can even be several degrees below the horizon. It is most accurate when the zenith distance of the sun is 90 degrees, and is seldom used when the sun is more than a few degrees from the horizon." (Bowditch 1962)

The basic principle of the sky compass is the polarization of light. The sky compass is of most value in high latitudes during twilight, when the sun is slightly below the horizon. Its accuracy decreases rapidly when the negative altitude of the sun exceeds about 6.5 degrees.

As stated above, it is most sensitive and accurate when the sun is near the horizon, the time when it is most needed.

The similarity between the function of the sky compass and the sunstone is obvious. Which mineral was available to the Vikings that would have had the same effect as the artificially produced Polaroid filter? The Iceland spar is one that will serve as a Polaroid filter. The earth's atmosphere serves as a polarizer and the Iceland spar serves as an analyzer.

The Kollsman sky compass was used principally in the polar region to correct the gyrocompass when the magnetic compass was unreliable or subject to large and erratic errors. In these regions, twilight lasts for hours, or at the poles, weeks; and the sun is seldom far from the horizon. Since its use is confined to periods of twilight, it is sometimes called a twilight compass.

The sky compass function is the same as the sunstone: it just has the addition of optical and measuring devices. In other words, old navigation became new navigation.

More can be found in a publication of the U.S. Navy Hydrographic Office; in their publication: *Air Navigation*, HO No. 216, 1995.

Appendix 3

A Comparison of the Oseberg and the Gokstad Viking Ships:

The Oseberg Ship is believed to be the burial ship of the great Viking Queen Aasa. It was found in 1903 in a burial mound on the southwestern coast of Norway. The ship was excavated in 1904, chemically preserved, and now is housed fully intact in the Vikingship Museum at Bygdøy outside of Oslo, Norway.

The Gokstad Viking Ship was discovered in 1880, buried in a huge mound of blue clay southwest of Oslo. The clay had preserved the oak vessel for 1000 years. It has been beautifully restored and is also on display at the Vikingship Museum.

The Oseberg and the Gokstad ships are similar. They more or less belong to the same class of ships, but the Gokstad ship is a bit longer and more solidly built.

The Oseberg ship was built entirely of oak. Its length is 71 feet (21.58 meters), with a beam of 16 feet (5.10 meters). The measurement from the railing to the keel amidships is 5 feet (1.58 meters). She was a large open ship equipped for both rowing and sailing. The ship was probably built as a royal yacht for coastwise voyaging and pleasure in good weather. Her last use was as a burial ship for Queen Aasa. Inside the ship, in the forward end they found furniture that had been buried with the queen. They also found oars, bailer, gangway, tubs, pails, and a working sled. The most striking characterization of the Oseberg ship is the high stem and stern with its very fine wood carving decoration of a sea dragon.

There was no trace of the sail, but all 15 pairs of oars were found in good shape. The oars are made of pine and the length varies from 12 feet (3.70 meters) to 14 feet (4.03 meters), all according to the distance between the oar ports and the surface of the water, which was greater at the bow and stern than amidships.

The oar ports were round holes in the side of the railing with slits across the center of the holes for the blades of the oars. The oar ports could be shut from the inside of the ship with small shutters to keep the water out when the ship was under sail.

(Adapted from *Viking Ships in Oslo* by Torleif Sjøvold)

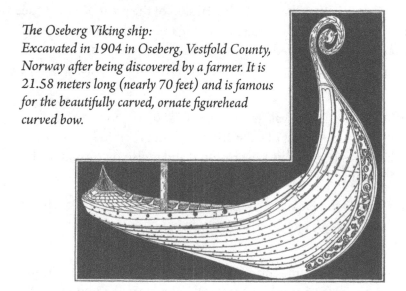

The Oseberg Viking ship:
Excavated in 1904 in Oseberg, Vestfold County,
Norway after being discovered by a farmer. It is
21.58 meters long (nearly 70 feet) and is famous
for the beautifully carved, ornate figurehead
curved bow.

Researchers think that the rowers must have used their sea chests to sit on when they rowed and taken them ashore when they left the ship, because no sea chests or rowing benches were found in the excavation of the Oseberg or the Gokstad ships. When the oars were not in use they could be stored in the large wooden forks which are placed in pairs on each side of the ship.

The Gokstad ship was also built of oak, with a much stronger keel. It is one solid piece. The length is 76 feet (23.24 meters), with a beam of 17 feet (5.2 meters). The measurement from the railing to the keel amidships is 7.2 feet (2.2 meters). The ship was outfitted with 16 pairs of oars. The construction of the Gokstad ship is much stronger than the Oseberg, which made it much more seaworthy.

The seaworthiness of the Gokstad ship was fully tested in 1893. A Norwegian replica of the Gokstad ship, the "Viking" was under command of Captain Magnus Andersen when he sailed from Bergen, Norway to Newfoundland in twenty-eight days. Andersen noted the flexibility of her hull. Leakage at the seams and through fastenings must always have been a problem, so bailing was a constant task on the original ships just as it is on the modern replicas.

The Gokstad ship was probably built shortly after the middle of the ninth century, a few years after the Oseberg. The Gokstad ship is a perfect example of an oceangoing ship, whereas the Oseberg is more suited for coastal use.

The Oseberg and the Gokstad ships are unlike the *knarr*. The *knarr* was a merchant ship built for cargo capacity and seaworthiness, and simpler in design. The *knarr* was relatively deeper and broader in the beam and made less speed than the long ships, the Oseberg and the Gokstad ships.

The design of the *knarr* came about when the need for such a vessel was demanded to transport the early settlers with their belongings to Iceland, Greenland, Faeroes, Shetland Islands, England, Isle of Man, Ireland and Scotland. The same type of ship was later used as a supply ship to and from the settlements.

Appendix 4

Replica Viking Ships "Saga Siglar" and "Borgundknarren":

In 1962, Roskilde museum found five ships under water in the Peberrende at Roskildefjord, Denmark. They named them "Skuldelevskibe" 1,2,3,4, and 5. Both "Saga Siglar"and "Borgundknarren" are true copies of the Skuldelevskibe 1. "Saga Siglar" was built in 1982-1983 by Sigurd Bjørkedalen and his sons. "Borgundknarren" was also built in Bjørkedalen by the same builders in 1992-1993. "Borgundknarren" was launched May 8, 1993. My wife June and I were there for the launching. "Borgundknarren" was built for Sunnmøre Museum in Ålesund, Norway.

Specifications of Replica Viking Ship "Borgundknarren"

Material used: Pine planking, oak for the keel, the curved fore-and-aft stems from a single piece of oak. The keelson, keel, steering oar and frames were also made out of oak.

Length overall	54 feet (16.5 meters)
Beam	15 feet (4.6 meters)
Height	6.2 feet (1.9 meters)
Draft of hull	4.3 feet (1.3 meters)
Depth of steering oar	5.2 feet (1.6 meters)
Displacement	26 tons (ballast and equipment 16 tons)
Ballast varies between 8-13 tons depending on weather and the voyage.	
Fresh water capacity	1200 liters
Mast height	42.6 feet (13 meters)
Mast thickness	12.5 inches (32 cm)
Crew	5-8
Average speed	5-6 knots

Both replicas were equipped with engines to handle generators, emergency pumps, and, radios. Power is also necessary to aid the ships in and out of busy ports, for maneuvering alongside crowded docks, and for when there is no wind.

Safety equipment:

12-person emergency raft and survival suits for everybody on board
Radio direction finder (RDF)
EPIRB (emergency position-indicating radio beacon)

Appendix 5

Finding Longitude Direct by the Shadow Pin Method:

I have been experimenting with the shadow pin for quite some time. The following calculation of longitude proves how accurate the shadow pin method is. For this, I of course need a watch, and the Nautical Almanac.

Compare the length of an afternoon shadow with that of the morning shadow. Use the shadow pin, a watch, and the Nautical Almanac. I have made several observations here in Port Orchard, Washington. Position: Lat. 47°34.5′N, Long. 122°34′W.

A shadow pin 6 cm high was used for the observation, (any height will work). The procedure was straight forward following the information from the earlier chapter in this book, *Finding True North by the Sun.*

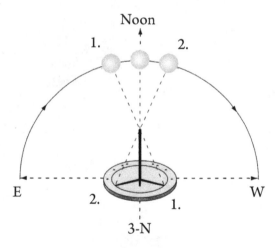

Finding true north by the sun
1: Before noon
2: After noon
3: Noon
(looking south)

Estimated: Finding meridian passage from the Nautical Almanac. Longitude 122° 34′W.

July 20th, 2002

Mer.pass. + DR longitude (W) = UT (GMT) of LAN

12h 06m + 08h 10m = 20h 16m UT

UT= Universal Time, LAN = Local Apparent Noon.

Meridian passage by the shadow pin method:

When I marked the first point, I also noticed the exact time: hours, minutes, and seconds. In the afternoon when the shadow again touched the circle, I marked the second point. Again I noticed the exact time. Midway between the two points lies the meridian. This will also be the north-south line.

While I was waiting for the shadow to touch the circle again, I periodically made marks as the shadow moved. When the shadow touched the circle again I made my final mark. These marks form a line. This line points from west to east, which gave me an east-west direction.

By the shadow method:

First shadow	19h 16m 00s GMT
Second shadow	21h 17m 20s GMT

19h 16m 00s + 21h 17m 20s = 40h 33m 20s

40h 33m 20s divided by 2 = 20h 16m 40s

When a body is on an observer's meridian, the longitude of the place is equal to the body's GHA in west longitude, and 360° - GHA in east longitude.

(GHA is an abbreviation for Greenwich Hour Angle, the difference in local time and Greenwich time expressed in degrees.)

GHA at 20h 16m 40s GMT = My longitude
From the Nautical Almanac 2002:

First I look up GHA for 20h GMT, July 20,
then look up increment for 16m 40s

20h GMT = 118° 24.5′
16m 40s =   4° 10.0′

122° 34.5′W

Longitude from the chart = 122° 34′ West. This is a difference of only 0.4 nautical miles, just as good as using a sextant or the GPS.

From the sagas we know the Vikings used the sun for navigation. They definitely could have used this method without the clock and the Nautical Almanac to get their north-south and east-west direction.

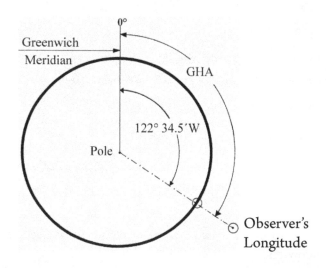

Appendix 6

The Definition of Dægr (length of a day):

In the thirteenth century the unknown Norwegian author of the "King's Mirror" (Konung's Skuggsjá) explained to his son about the question of time. On the question of time and its division, the author of the "King's Mirror" seems to have had nearly all the information that the age possessed. He explained about "dægra sigling" and "dægr".

"Sjau dægra sigling: a sail of seven days between Norway and Iceland." (Quote: Dictonary of Old Icelandic, Oxford at the Clarendon Press 1926).

"Dægr: He divides the period of day and night into two 'days' (dægr)of twelve hours each." (This statement has created controversy and disagreement among scholars.)

The definition of dægr: *"One half of the astronomical day, twelve hours of the day or night. An astronomical day; twenty-four hours."* (Quote: Dictonary of old Icelandic, Oxford at the Clarendon Press 1926)

The Norwegian author might have written down this statement during the Equinoxes, because that is the only time that day and night are approximately twelve hours each.

The Equinoxes are the two days of the year when the sun crosses the equator. The vernal (spring) equinox—on or about March 21 in modern times—is when the sun's declination changes from south to north. The autumn equinox—on or about September 23 in modern times—is when the declination changes from north to south. On the Equinoxes, the sun rises due east and sets due west, remaining above the horizon for 12 hours. The word "Equinox," meaning "equal nights," is applied because it occurs at the time when days and nights are of approximately equal length all over the earth. (Bowditch Pub. No. 9, 1999)

In Old Norse, the word "dægr" is used. In modern Icelandic the word "Dægur" is listed in the Icelandic dictionary as day or night, twelve hours.

Now back to the King's Mirror.

In this statement: "As for how long an hour should be I can give you definite information; for there should be twenty-four hours in two days, that is, a night and a day, while the sun courses through the eight primary points of the sky: and according to right reckoning the sun will pass through each division in three hours of the day."

Thus the hour is defined as one-twenty-fourth part of the two "days" (day and night) that comprise one cycle of light and dark.

In modern terminology:

"The sun appears to move westward around the earth once a day, crossing over 360° of longitude every 24 hours. Which means the sun moves west at a rate of 15° of longitude per hour." (Burch, 1990.)

1 primary division = 3 hours

and

1 primary division = 45°

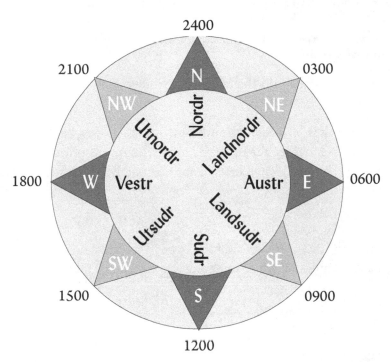

The primary points of the Viking twenty-four hour day, referenced to *áttir* directions.

2400	Miðnætti	midnight
0300	Ótta	3 am
0600	Miður morgunn	6 am
0900	Dagmál	9 am
1200	Hádegi	12 noon
1500	Nón, udorn, *eykt**	3 pm
1800	Miðaftan	6 pm
2100	Náttmál	9 pm

*Grágás 1: "Latin *nonae* (originally 1500 hours) and *eykt* seems to have come to define about the same time: 1500 to 1530 hours."

Appendix 7

Visible Range of Land:

The curvature of the earth limits the range of sight regardless of the clarity of the atmosphere.

If a mountain peak is "H" feet high and someone is standing "h" feet above the water, then he will first see the tip of the mountain on the horizon (in clear weather and calm seas) when located approximately "D" nautical miles from the peak.

$$D = \sqrt{H} + \sqrt{h}$$

The mountain top 1521 feet high could have been seen just on the horizon at about 42 nautical miles off when someone was standing 9 feet above the water.

$$D = \sqrt{1521} + \sqrt{9}$$
$$D = 39 + 3$$
$$D = 42 \text{ nautical miles}$$

Note that this works only with feet and nautical miles.

(Adapted from the book *Emergency Navigation* By David Burch 1990.)

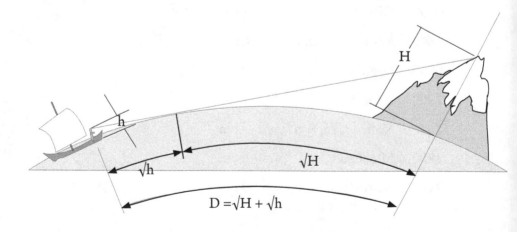

Appendix 8

Climate Change in the Greenland Area of the Arctic:

Scientific studies and ice core samples from the Greenland glaciers give evidence that during the years from 700-1350, the years of Viking exploration and settlement in Greenland and Iceland, the climate in these regions was much warmer than it is today. The evidence of the warm era is further found in sediment cores from the Nansen Fjord of the eastern coast of Greenland. These sediment cores show there was a warm and very stable climate in the region from the 8th through the 12th centuries. This means that the sea ice would not likely be a hindrance for Viking ships when they traveled between Iceland and Greenland. Studies of fossil pollen and vegetation records of the Scandinavian countries and across northern Europe also support these conclusions. These studies further show that immediately after this balmy era there followed the coldest period to occur in the last seven hundred years.

The warm and stable period was conducive to the exploration and settlement of the Arctic and sub-Arctic regions. When the climate abruptly changed the fjords and bays became clogged with ice. Supply ships to the Greenland settlements could not get through. This was probably the biggest factor in the ultimate failure of the Greenland settlements, and perhaps the outposts in North America. (*Vikings : The North Atlantic Saga*, National Museum of Natural History, US).

In 1984 captain Ragnar Thorset, his family, and crew set out on a trip from Norway to sail around the world in an open Viking ship, a *knarr*, the "Saga Siglar." When they left Iceland for Greenland the plan was to sail through the Ikerassua (Prins Christian Sound). Ikerassua is a deep and narrow sound that forms an east-west passage north of Kap Farvel at the southern tip of Greenland. But ice reports showed that the sound was full of pack ice, and impossible to sail through. Even ships especially built for sailing in icy waters had to sail around the Kap Farvel area. Another disappointment was waiting for them. The drift ice was compacted solidly for about one-hundred nautical miles south of Kap Farvel, and the whole Julianehåb bay was full of ice as well. It was impossible for the Saga Siglar to sail into Austurbyggð where Eirik the Red settled. If Eirik had met ice conditions like this, it would have been doubtful that they would have been able to enter the harbor, therefore they wouldn't have settled there at all.

Normally the pack-ice has cleared out by August, but some years have more ice than others. If there is any ice in the eastern entrance, the sound will usually be blocked. The Saga Siglar continued around Kap Farvel but further south out to sea, all the way to Latitude 58° 30' N and 44° West. This was the end of the pack ice. They headed north again until they were abeam Nuuk (Godthåb) and Vesturbyggð and finally made into port at Nuuk.

Captain Thorseth's voyage and the scientific research with ice core samples shows how much the climatic conditions have changed since Viking times. Places that were then attractive to the Viking settlers cannot now even be reached, and climatic conditions in many areas, especially Greenland, are marginal for settlements. *(Saga Siglar Forlis — Vikingenas seilas, 1993)*

Somewhat related to climate is the fact that the level of the North Atlantic Ocean was about two to two and a half feet higher in the Viking era than at present. This would not have affected the passages from land to land but did change the shoreline and the width of the mouths of rivers and fjords.

Appendix 9

Regiment of the Pole:

It has been known to navigators since ancient times that the alignment of the Big Dipper "pointer" stars could be used to find Polaris, on the tip of the Little Dipper's handle. It is, however, always the location of the invisible celestial pole (true north)—about which all the stars all circling once a day—that is needed for navigation, not the location of Polaris.

Polaris was about 6° away from the celestial pole in Viking times; the navigator needed a way to determine the distance of this offset of Polaris from true north. This knowledge is needed for finding accurate direction relative to north, or for determining and keeping track of latitude.

Rules and instruments for making this evaluation were common in the textbooks of the 1500s, and the methodology with the Little Dipper was referred to in ancient Greek documents. In 16th Century texts, these rules were referred to as "The Regiment of the Pole" (at that time Polaris was offset by 3° 30').

The key in Viking times would have been, for example, to learn by observation that whenever the cup of the Little Dipper is parallel to the horizon, "ready to catch water," the true pole of the sky is located 6° due east of Polaris that is, the pole is at the same altitude as Polaris, 6° to the right. This orientation would give one element of the Regiment: "when the cup is on the table," your latitude equals the height of Polaris and Polaris bears 6° West of North. Twelve hours later, we get another element of the Regiment: "when the cup is emptying water," the pole and the star are again at the same elevation, but now Polaris is 6° to the east of the pole (north). Other elements might be (six hours before the latter), "when the cup is standing up," the latitude is 6° larger than the elevation of the Polaris and the bearing of the Polaris is true north. Twelve hours later, "when the Cup is standing on its head," the latitude is 6° lower than the elevation of Polaris and Polaris is again bearing due north. Corrections at other times of night would have been estimated from these.

For pure latitude sailing, however, it is only the general principle that matters. Knowledge of the precise value of the offset is not needed (although it is not at all difficult to measure when on land). The navigation trick would be to simply note the height of Polaris at a home port (say 64°N) at a particular orientation of the Little Dipper at twilight during the sailing season. Then if they wanted to cross the ocean at 61° North, they would head south along the coast until they "sailed down the altitude" of Polaris to what they wanted. The farther south they go, the lower Polaris would be, providing they always measured its height at the same time of day. This was determined by the orientation of the Little Dipper, being the same as it was when they measured at their home port.

It does not matter if the actual correction is 6° or 0° or anything in between. The measurement is relative to that of the home port of known latitude. When the star has descended by 3°, they know they are where they want to depart from.

Accurate (relative) star elevations of 60° or so are not difficult to improvise on shore, but these are much more difficult at sea without proper instruments. In very calm conditions, they might obtain an accuracy of 2° or so, which might get them to a rather large target zone (visible range of mountain peaks, ranges of land, birds, etc.) at the end of a voyage. But for more precise, stellar position navigation, they had to rely on stars at much lower altitudes. It is much easier to measure the elevations of low "horizon skimming stars," even with makeshift instruments. Sailing at high latitudes presents a unique opportunity for such star sightings, which we propose was indeed one of the secrets of Viking navigation.

(Adapted from the methods proposed in the book *Emergency Navigation*, by David Burch.)

Glossary

Aft   Towards the stern.

Aktaumr (braces)   Long sheets leading aft from the ends of the yardarm. They are used to square the yard, turning the sail, and steady the yard during sailing. The braces are controlled from the ship's after deck.

Athwartship   At right angle to the fore and aft line of a vessel.

Áttir   Division of the Old Norse horizon (360°) into eight main directions.

Åttering   Boat used primarily for short coastal trips, powered by sail or oars; capacity about 12 persons.

Beamy   A vessel of wide proportion relative the length; sturdy; not easily capsized.

Beitiás (tackpole)   Wooden pole that transfers some of the tremendous energy from the hals (tack) to the hull.

Bow   The forward part of a vessel.

Boline (bowline)   The bowline is attached to the forward vertical edge on the square sail. It is secured about 1/3 up from the foot of the sail.

Ballast   A quantity of any weighted material, usually stones, placed in the hull of the vessel to increase the stability by lowering the center of gravity. Used when there is little or no cargo on board.

Belaying pin   A device made of brass, iron, or wood used to fasten lines.

Broaching   A position of the ship broadside to the waves and a condition to be avoided. In heavy weather with following seas, if steering control is lost and the vessel broaches, it may capsize.

Calcite (see Iceland spar).

Daegr Length of the day.

Dead reckoning (DR)   The estimate of a ship's position by using the courses steered and the distance run.

Dragreip (halyard)   A line used to hoist and lower the yard and sail.

Dybdelodd (see lead).

Faering   Smaller rowboat carried on knarr vessels for use in port or for emergencies at sea.

Fair wind   A wind which aids a sailing ship in making progress in a desired direction.

Freeboard   The vertical distance from the deck of a vessel to the surface of the water, usually measured amidships.

Gale   A strong wind, less powerful than a storm. Gale measures wind force 8 on the Beaufort wind scale (34 to 40 knots).

Half-vind   Wind coming from the from side (beam) of the ship.

Hals (tack)   The sheet holding down the lower forward corner of the sail; it is controlled from the forward end of the ship.

Hafship   An ocean going Viking ship.

Iceland spar (also known as optical calcite, or silfurberg)   Calcium carbonate mineral possessing a rhombohedral crystal structure. Its opposite faces are parallel but there are no right angles. A perfect crystal is colorless and transparent. Optical calcite possesses the unique ability to split one ray of light into two rays of light, otherwise known as double refraction.

Keel   Main framing member of hull, along the center line from bow to stern, to which the frames are attached.

Knarr   A high sided, broad built ocean going sailing vessel used to carry cargo and passengers in the Norway - Iceland - Greenland trade, and other places the Viking sailed.

Landfall   The position of the first land sighted in coming in from the sea.

Leeward   Toward the lee, or in the general direction away from the source of the wind. The opposite is windward.

Leeway   The angle that the ship moves off course in the downwind direction, and it is the difference between the ship's heading (the course steered) and the course actually sailed.

Leads   A weight attached to a line used to determining depth of water. There are two types of lead - the hand lead and the deep-sea (pronounced dipsey) lead. The former is used in shallow water and weight of either 7 or 14 lbs., the dipsey lead for soundings up to a hundred fathoms, with weight of 50 to 100 lbs.

Latitude sailing   The Viking practice of first sail to the latitude of the destination along the coast, and then follow this parallel until landfall was made.

Port   The left side of a ship, facing forward. The opposite is STARBOARD.

Priar   There are several variations of the priar. On smaller sail, it is a single line leading to a three-legged rooster foot at the center of the foot of the sail. The other end is made fast to the mast. On larger square sails, such as the one on the "Borgundknarren," it is used as described in the text.

Rå   A square sail.

Rakki   A piece of wood shaped like a horseshoe, its main purpose is to keep the yardarm close to the mast.

Reef To decrease the sail's area. The square sail is partly lowered and the surplus sail is rolled up and secured by a band of reef points placed parallel with the foot of the sail.

Reef Points Short pieces of small rope, set in the reef bands of the sail for reefing purposes.

Scree Loose rock debris; usually a sloping area at the base of a steep incline of cliff.

Sea anchor An object towed by a vessel, to keep the vessel's stern to a heavy sea, done to reduce the speed of the ship, and to decrease the possibility of broaching.

Sheet (line) Rope attached to sail or yardarm used to adjust the sail's angle to the wind.

Shroud The eight lines, four on each side, used to support the mast. These are attached from the top of the mast to the frames of the ship.

Siglu Sail.

Siglure (yardarm) A beam crossing a mast horizontally from which a square sail is set.

Siglutre Mast.

Skaut (lower sheet) The sheet holding down the lower aft corner of the sail. The name changes (hals or skaut) depending on which tack is set. The skaut is controlled from the ship's afterdeck.

Starboard The right side of a ship, facing forward. The opposite is PORT.

Stern The after part of a vessel.

Storm Wind force 10 on the Beaufort wind scale (48 to 55 knots).

Tack To turn the bow through the wind.

Tiller A handle use to direct the rudder. Viking ships used an athwartship tiller, attached at right angle to a side rudder through a hole in the upper part of the side rudder. The handle is about 3 to 4 feet long.

Wadmal Wool fabric for sails noted for its strength and durability.

Zenith The point on the celestial sphere vertically overhead.

Bibliography:

Bowditch, Nathaniel. *The American Practical Navigator*, Washington D.C.: Pub. No. 9: 1962.
The encyclopedia of marine navigation on all waters. It includes a brief section on lifeboat navigation and valuable information on oceanography and weather.

Burch, David. *Inland and Coastal Navigation: For Power-Driven and Sailing Vessels*. Second Edition. Starpath Publications, Seattle, WA, 2014. www.starpath.com.

Burch, David. *Celestial Navigation: A Complete Home Study Course*. Second Edition. Starpath Publications, Seattle, WA, 2016. www.starpath.com.

Burch, David. *Emergency Navigation*, International Marine, 1990.

Bunn, W. Charles. *Crystals, Their Role in Nature and Science*. New York Academic Press,1964

Christensen, Arne-Emil. *Vikingenes Verdensbilde*, Shipsbygging og Navigation Oslo, Norsk Sjøfartsmuseum, 1992

Chandlers, S. Robbins, Bertel Bruun, and Herbert S. Zim. *Birds of North America*, Golden Press New York, 1983

Blindheim, Joan Tindale, *Vinland The Good*. Engers Boktrykkeri A/S Otta, Norway, 1986.

Den Norske Los, *The Norwegian Pilot*. Sailing Directions Bergen-Statt. The Norwegian Hydrographic Service. First edition, Stavanger, Norway, 1990.

The Kongelige Nordisk Oldskrift-Selskab. København, Denmark. *Landnámabók*. Thiels Bogtrykkeri, 1900.

Gross, Grant M., *Oceanography, a view of the earth*, Second edition. Prentice-Hall, Inc. Englewood Cliffs, NJ 07632, 1977.

Holland, Hjalmar R., *Explorations in America Before Columbus*, Second edition. Twayne Publishers, New York, 1958.

Hoyt, Erich, *The Whales of Canada*. An Equinox Wildlife Handbook, Camden East, Ontario KOK 1HO, Canada, 1950.

H.O. North Coast of Scotland Pilot, second edition. Published by the Hydrographer of the Navy. Taunton Somerset, England. North and North-East Coast of Scotland from Cape Wrath to Rattray Head and including Caledonian Canal, Orkney Island, Shetland Islands, and Føroyar (Faeroe Islands), 1994.

H.O. Pub. 216. United States Government Printing Office, Washington, DC, 1955.

Huygens, Christiaan, *Treatise on Light.* University of Chicago Press

Kyselka, Will, and Ray Lanterman, *North Star to Southern Cross.* Honolulu: The University Press of Hawaii, 1976.

Kals, W.S., *Stars and Planets,* Sierra Club, 730 Polk Street, San Francisco, CA 94109, 1990.

La Fay, Howard, *The Vikings.* National Geographic Society, 1145 17th Street NW Washington, DC 20036, 1972

Larson, Laurens, *The King's Mirror* (Konungs Skuggsjá). The American-Scandinavian Foundation London. Humphrey Milford Oxford University Press, 1917.

Laws of early Iceland, Grágás. University of Manitoba, Winnipeg, Canada, 1980.

Lewis, David,*We, the Navigators: The ancient art of Landfinding in the Pacific,* Second edition, University of Hawaii Press, 1994

Lyman, Dave, *Pitch and Roll in Polynesian Seafaring Heritage,* Kamehameha Schools Press, Honolulu, 1980.

Magnusson & Pálsson, *The Vinland Sagas.* Penguin Books Ltd., 27 Wrights Lane, London W8 5TZ, England 1964.

McGrew Julia, *Sturlunga Saga.* 2 volumes, Twayne Pub. Inc. New York, 1974.

Nordlandsbåten og Åfjordsbåten. Gunnar Eldjarn og John Godal. A.Kjellands Forlag A.S, Lesja, Norway, 1988

Paine, Stefani, *The Nature of Arctic Whales.* Greystone Books, A division of Douglas and McIntyre LTD., Vancouver, BC, V51 2H1, Canada, 1995.

Pearson, T.H., *Journal of Animal Ecology*, 1968.

Ramskou, Thorkild, *Solstenen: Vikingernes Kompas*. Copenhagen: Rhodos, 1969.

Rinman, Thorsten, *I Vaesterled*. Utgiven av Svensk Sjöfarts Tidning Tryckt 1995. Novum Grafiska AB, Göteborg, Sweden, 1995.

Saga Siglar Forlis Vikingenes Seilaser, Authors: Ragnar Thorseth, Helge Ingstad, Arvid Bryne, Jan F. Midtflá, Peter Daniel Baade, Elizabeth Løvold Pedersen, Publisher: Nordvest Forlag AS, Fløttmannsgata 2, 6004, Alesund, Norway, 1992

Shaw, David, *Flying Cloud: The True Story of America's Most Famous Clipper Ship and the Woman Who Guided Her*, Harper Collins, NY, 2001

Swaney, Deanna, *Iceland, Greenland, and the Faeroe Islands, a Travel Survival Kit*. Lonely Planet Publications. P.O. Box 617 Hawthorn, Vic. 3122, Australia, 1994.

Thirslund, S., *Viking Navigation*, Gullanders Bogtrykkeri a-s, Skjern, Denmark, 1998.

Tennissen, Anthony C., *Nature of Earth Materials*, 2nd edition, Prentice Hall, Englewood Cliffs, NJ, 1983.

Thornhill and Major W. W. Ker, RCC Pilotage Foundation, *Faeroe, Iceland, and Greenland. Cruising Notes*. Imray Laurie Norie & Wilson Ltd., Cambridgeshire, PE17 4BT, England, 1995.

Vadstrup, Søren, *I Vikingernes Kølvand*, Vikingskibshallen I Roskilde, Denmark, 1993.

Vebaek, C. L., and Thirslund, S. *The Viking Compass*, Gullanders Bogtrykkeri a-s, Skjern, Denmark, 1992.

Van Dorn, William G., *Oceanography and Seamanship*, Dodd Mead and Company, New York, 1974.

Vikings: The North Atlantic Saga, William W. Fitzhugh, National Museum of

Natural History, Elisabeth I. Ward (Editors), American Museum of Natural History, New York, 2001.

Nordlandsbåten and Åfjordsbåten by Gunnar Eldjarn og John Godal Bind 1, Page 92, A.Kjellands Forlag A.S, Lesja, Norway, 1988.

The Viking Ships of Oslo by Thorleif Sjøvold, University Oldsaksamling, Oslo, 1985.

Internet References:

The Viking Sun Compass
www.griffithobs.org/IPSViking.html

Starpath School of Navigation
www.starpath.com

Grettir the Strong, an Icelandic Saga
www.hn.psu.edu/faculty/jmanis/grettir.htm

Icelandic literature
www.lysator.liu.se/nordic/scn/faq55.html

Vikings the North Atlantic Saga (Smithsonian)
www.mnh.si.edu/vikings/start.html

Viking Net
www.vikingship.net

Nordic Photos
www.nordicphotos.com

Photography and illustration credits:

Pages 4, 126: Nordic Stock.

Pages 169, 170, 173, and back cover photo by June Garrett-Groshong.

Pages 79, 80, 83, 85 86, 91, 93, 94, 97, 98, 101, 105, 107, 109, 151 drawing and diagrams by Leif K. Karlsen.

Page 76 photo courtesy: David Burch.

Photos of pages from the sagas courtesy: Ólöf Benediktsdóttir, Librarian, Arni Magnusson Institute, Reykjavik, Iceland.

Title page photo of Leif Eiriksson, sunstone photos, all other illustrations: Marlin Greene.

Illustrations aboard ship based on photographs aboard the replica Viking-ship "Vidfamne" from Gothenburg, Sweden.

Courtesy photographer: Ove Laange, Sweden.

Page 52 photo used for illustration courtesy: David Foster.

Page 64 photo of replica ship "Icelander" used for illustration courtesy: Captain Gunnar Maril Eggertsson.

Index

A

adz 8,18
Akraberg 138
Alkaid 108
Arnarfjord 78
Áttir 85
Austr 85

B

backstay 9
Baffin Island 120,148
beam 29
beamy 8
Beinisvörd Ciffs 139
beitiás 11,32,56,70,71
Big Dipper 29
Bishop Gudmund 78
Bjarni Herjulfsson 37
Borgafjord 132
Borgund*knarre*n 69
Bowditch 95,104,180,189,200
Breidafjord 132

C

calcite 78,80,176
Capella 108
Cape Cod 150
Cape Horn 102
Catherine Carlson 148
Christiaan Huygens 81
Christians 17
close-hauled 69
coins 16,49
Columbus 120
crystal 26

D

Dagmal 87
Danell fjord 134
David Burch 95
dipsey 35

Dr. Helge Ingstad 120

E

Eastern settlement 131
Eirik the Red 37
Erasmus Bartholimus 81
Eykt 85-87,115,152,154
eyktarstad 87,150-53

F

færing 19,47,48,53
Faeroe Islands 85
falcons 15,51,53
forestay 9,10
Fredriksdal 132
freeboard 8,10
Frohavet 21
fulmars 33

G

gannets 33
Garðskagi 54
Geirfálki 9,12,14,17,22,36,47,49,55,58
Gibraltar 147
gimbal 55,97
Gísli Sigurðsson 149
Glaciers
   Eyafjalljökull 46
   Kronprins Fredriks 130
   Mýrdalsjökull 46
   Örafajökull 35
   Vatnajökull 33,35,123,125,126,127
Glaumbær 120
Godthåb 132
Gray Goose 59
Greenland 37,67
Gulathing Law 59
Gulf of Saint Lawrence 150

205

Printed in the USA
CPSIA information can be obtained
at www.ICGtesting.com
LVHW091553191123
764359LV00004B/367